LETTERS FROM

Letters from Long Kesh

DES O'HAGAN

CITIZEN PRESS

Originally published in newspaper column style in
The Irish Times during 1972

Published in thiss book format by
Citizen Press
2012

48 North Great George's St,
Dublin 1
Tel: 01 - 8733 916

6 Springfield Road
Belfast BT12 7AG
Tel: 028 - 90 328 663

ISBN 978-0-9572835-0-3

Typeset by Citizen Press
Printed in Ireland

CONTENTS

Introduction

A T FOUR AM ON the morning of August 9. 1971, the
Royal Ulster Constabulary and the British Army
implemented Operation Demetrius – internment – on the
orders of the Ulster Unionist Prime Minister of Northern
Ireland, Brian Faulkner, backed by the Tory government
in London. Across Northern Ireland, armoured cars
roared into streets, doors were kicked in, people were
dragged from their beds by always aggressive and often
abusive soldiers, terrifying the targeted families. The
security forces were working off a list of four hundred and
fifty names that had been drawn up by the RUC Special
Branch and MI5. Three hundred and forty two people
were detained; many of them were not even on the list.
The operation was a disaster by any yardstick.

In security terms, it failed to capture many of its targets,
or to seriously damage the structures of the Republican
Movement or the Provisionals. The worst violence since
August 1969 followed, with seventeen people killed over
the following forty eight hours. The majority were civilians
murdered by the British army, most especially in
Ballymurphy (where eleven civilians were killed from

August 9 to 11). Thousands of people fled their homes, and community tensions worsened. Politically, internment proved that the Unionist regime at Stormont, that had bitterly resisted the demands for civil rights and attempted to baton early civil rights marches off the streets, would not accept the extension of full democratic rights to its opponents. Instead, it would govern through the notorious Special Powers Act. Despite Brian Faulkner's claim that Demetrius was an operation targeted solely at 'violent men', the list of those interned reveals the more reactionary and sectarian reality. Every single person interned on August 9 was an anti-Unionist. Not one unionist – violent or otherwise – was targeted. The government interned a broad range of its opponents, most especially people who were active in the Northern Ireland Civil Rights Association and the civil rights campaign. Among those from the NICRA Executive arrested were its Chairman Ivan Barr and NICRA's organiser, Kevin McCorry. Many members of the Republican Clubs who were arrested were also prominent in NICRA. It is hard to say whether they were targeted for their belief in a socialist republic or their belief in civil rights for everyone in Northern Ireland. Internment widened the breach between the Stormont regime and its opponents, who quickly withdrew cooperation with the state in protest. Politicians withdrew from public bodies and local councils (the SDLP had already withdrawn from Stormont after the British army lied about shooting two unarmed men dead in Derry), while a mass rents and rates strike demonstrated the popular opposition to internment. The mass campaign against internment made it clear that the

Stormont regime had lost any semblance of legitimacy in the eyes of its opponents, and the removal of Stormont and imposition of direct rule became simply a matter of time.

TED HEATH AND THE Tories assumed power in June 1970. They brought with them a desire to prove that they remained the party of law and order as well as close ties to the Ulster Unionist Party, which was demanding more robust action against its opponents. The Tories were also more sympathetic than Labour to the most reactionary elements of the British security services, whose thoughts were dominated by the Cold War. They believed less in negotiation and reform, and more in the use of force. The consequences of this general policy of getting tough were soon seen in Oman, in Northern Ireland, and in relations with the trade unions in Britain. As noted in the publication, *The Story of the Falls Curfew*, the Tories instantly began adopting a harder line in Northern Ireland, giving the military a freer hand. One of the first results was the illegal Falls Road curfew, which saw the murder of civilians, the wrecking of homes and the mass violation of the civil rights of thousands of inhabitants by the British army. This new attitude resulted in the following years in many civilian deaths at the hands of soldiers who invariably claimed that their admitted victims were armed. On other occasions, they sought to deny responsibility. The memoirs of Sergeant Ray Derrick detail him being given twenty rounds off the record by his commanding officer so that if his men killed anybody during Operation Demetrius in Derry they would be able to deny it by each returning to base with the number of rounds they had been officially issued. During Bloody Sunday, at least one soldier fired more rounds than he had been issued, suggesting that Derrick's experience was part of a pattern. The Tories placed their faith in repression.

Brian Faulkner became Prime Minister of Northern Ireland in March 1971. Faulkner at this time had a fairly hard-line reputation. Despite some indications that he was trying to be more moderate (such as appointing the former Northern Ireland Labour Party member David Bleakley as Minister for Community Relations), he believed that a security response was the most important element to solving the problems in Northern Ireland. The most reactionary elements of unionism, as represented by the likes of Bill Craig, had been calling for a security response to challenges to the Stormont regime since the early civil rights marches. They could not conceive of the idea that the state could tolerate opposition to its existence and methods from republicans and socialists and survive – this helps explain why the majority of those targeted for interment were from the Republican Movement, NCIRA, and the left generally. People like Craig believed that internment had defeated the Border Campaign in the 1950s (when it had been introduced on both sides of the border). It took on an almost magical significance for them – simply apply it, and all would be right in their world again. They had learnt nothing from Duke Street, Burntollet, August 1969, or the Falls curfew. Ian Paisley, on the other hand, opposed internment, something that made it more attractive to his Ulster Unionist opponents who were seeking to fight off the Paisleyite electoral challenge. It was the Ulster Unionists under Faulkner who pushed for internment the hardest, and they succeeded in convincing the Tories that it was necessary.

Internment, then, did not come about as a sudden panicked response to an upswing in violence, or anti-state agitation. It was part of a broader shift within British and Stormont government policy which downplayed the deep-rooted problems of Northern Ireland, and the need for substantial political reform, in favour of a strategy of minor concessions and repression. This attitude sprang from a number of factors, including the Tory desire to be seen as a tough government; the refusal of unionists to face up to the reality of the need for reform and their desire to crush opposition; the belief among the political and security establishment that the socialism of the Republican Movement made it the main threat to Northern Ireland; and a sense of desperation among unionists that the existence of the Stormont government, and the state itself was under threat, if they were unable to restore 'law and order'. The consequence of the Unionist Party's gamble on internment was to increase opposition, stimulate violence, and prove within a few months that the Stormont regime was no longer sustainable.

INTERNMENT WAS INTRODUCED UNDER the Special Powers Act. This notorious Act gained its highest praise when a minister from apartheid South Africa said that he would swap all the repressive legislation in South Africa for one clause of the Special Powers Act. The removal of the Special Powers Act was as much an aim of NICRA as one man, one vote, and an end to discrimination in jobs and housing. Internment in and of itself was a violation of civil rights – the use of the Special Powers Act only highlighted that fact. The abuse of the internees' civil rights, however, did not stop at the fact of internment. The British Army took the opportunity to indulge in some experimentation at psychological torture, while more traditional forms of brutality were also employed. Internment was used by the security forces as an opportunity to test the effects of the sensory deprivation using the 'five techniques' – wall standing (forcing people lean against a wall with all their weight on their fingers), hooding, subjection to 'white noise', sleep deprivation and deprivation of food and drink. The twelve 'hooded men' were subjected to this treatment for a week. The British government was later convicted by the European Court of Human Rights for *'inhuman and degrading treatment'* of these men, and London admitted its guilt. The techniques were declared illegal by the Parker report. Others, in Girdwood barracks, were forced to run barefoot across broken glass and rough stones, were threatened with dogs, kicked into a helicopter, and forced to jump out fifteen seconds later, before being forced to crawl back to the barracks while being kicked and punched.

These facts quickly reached the media. The British government instituted an inquiry, which was published in November 1971 as the Compton Report. The report was a whitewash. For example, it suggested that one of the hooded men, Paddy Joe McClean, had chosen to marinate in his own clothes rather than being denied the use of the toilet. It also accepted the military's claims that the incident with the helicopter was part of a deception operation to fool any observers into thinking that internees were being flown out of the barracks. This decision was reached on the basis of an 'independent' RAF witness who denied that he had seen the maltreatment described. However, the report did conclude that even what the inquiry accepted did happen 'under these circumstances does constitute a measure of ill-treatment.' As Des O'Hagan – who endured the helicopter incident and being forced to walk across stones barefoot at Gridwood – now notes: 'one must admire the British sense of distinction.'

I N August 1971, Des O'Hagan was a senior lecturer in sociology in Stranmillis College living in St Alban's Gardens in south Belfast. Having grown up in a house in Divis Street in the Lower Falls in Belfast where progressive politics where regularly discussed, he joined the Republican Movement as a teenager, and has remained politically active since then, whether at home or while a student in England at the London School of Economics. A founder member of the Northern Ireland Civil Rights Association, he was a member of its executive. A Marxist-Leninist, he was also a leading member of the Republican Clubs in Belfast, and was playing a prominent role, along with the likes of Cathal Goulding, Seán

Garland, Liam McMillen and Tomás MacGiolla, in the process that was transforming the Republican Movement into The Workers' Party. His high profile as a civil rights and republican activist guaranteed him the close attention of Special Branch and made him a natural target for internment when it was introduced.

Des O'Hagan was at home with his wife Marie and baby son when the soldiers of Operation Demetrius came knocking at the door. Having kicked the door in, they dragged him out – 'I barely had time to put on a shirt and pants' – barefoot. The nature of the arrest was such that one of the soldiers later returned to Marie, who had been holding a crying baby as her husband was dragged out of the house, and confessed that he had had felt like a Nazi in the Warsaw ghetto during the arrest. Des was taken from the local station to Girdwood Barracks where, having thrown him to the ground, each passing soldier took the opportunity to kick him in the small of the back. He suffers from back pain to this day. However one soldier soon protected him from the other soldiers and warned him not to go to the toilet on his own. His safety was also the cause of concern for several other prisoners. Standing beside a leading member of People's Democracy as they watched Des being placed up against a wall opposite soldiers cocking their rifles, Harry McKeown commented, 'Christ, they're going to shoot O'Hagan', at which point the PD man fainted.

On being moved from Girdwood, Des was the last man in the last group of prisoners moved out, walking in a straight line. An officer casually remarked to a soldier under his command, 'Put a bullet through O'Hagan's head and you'll kill the rest as well.' The threats and intimidation were far from over. A warder who knew Des protected him from two RUC men who wanted to separate him from the other internees. He told him to lock himself in a cubicle, and stayed outside furiously rowing with the RUC men until they left, promising that they would get O'Hagan at some point.

Des would be interned for a year and a day. His political activities, however, continued unabated. Having arrived at Long Kesh, he quickly helped found a Long Kesh branch of NICRA and he was an active member of the Republican Clubs there too. For example: in November 1971, in a letter he sent as the NICRA branch press officer to a public meeting against internment from what he and others termed 'Long Kesh Concentration Camp', he argued that the Unionist Party was fighting its last anti-democratic battle. 'For 50 years they have denied basic human rights. For almost a third of that time they have used internment against those who dissent from their views. This must be the last occasion that they have the opportunity to terrorise the community. The Special Powers Act must go.'

If Des continued to oppose the state during the loss of his liberty through internment, the state continued to pursue its campaign against him. He was in fact on bail when he was interned on a charge of possessing illegal documents. These documents were application forms to join the Republican Clubs. The magistrate fined him what he described as a nominal sum of £25, and gave him ten weeks to pay. He was then taken back to Long Kesh despite having answered his case in court. He was one of a number of internees charged for possessing documents and newspapers published by Sinn Féin and the Provisionals - despite the fact that the *United Irishman* and the like freely circulated within Long Kesh itself! Des in fact appeared in court twice while being interned. In March 1972, he appeared in court charged with the non-payment of rates. He explained that he was not paying the rates as a protest against 'the anti-democratic character of our society;' described the case as a 'sick joke' and argued that it demonstrated that the courts were themselves subject to political and party decisions. If these cases were petty harassment of political dissent, the loss of his job at the behest of a unionist politician was much more serious for a man with a family.

As well as participating as far as possible in politics outside the camp, Des and others like Frank McGlade and Art McMillen set about raising their own political consciousness and that of those around them. This involved acquiring and reading suitable books which were donated by sympathisers outside. It also included discussion groups, which would often go on until all hours of the night, and debates with people from different political positions. Some of these debates are alluded to in the letters that follow, but at their most bitter, they could take on a vicious edge. This was demonstrated most clearly when, during a debate about republicanism and anti-sectarianism, Gerry Adams commented that he would wade up to his knees in protestant blood for the Republic, while other Provisionals dismissed NICRA and the civil rights campaign as a distraction they wanted out of the way.

In Long Kesh, then, Des O'Hagan and others continued their work as civil rights activists and members of the Republican Clubs as far as possible. Limited though their access to information and material was, they participated in the campaigns for their own freedom, and for the full democratisation of Northern Ireland, as well as the promotion of unity among the working class. These debates had a lasting impact upon the development of the Republican Movement and then The Workers' Party in the years that followed.

THE TWENTY TWO LETTERS from Long Kesh, published in *The Irish Times* from January 1972 to July 1972, are a unique and extremely rich source for the political and social history of internment. Although people have written of their time in the internment camps after the event, they are unique as a sustained account of life within the camps written at the time. They address many of the major events and issues from the period – the reaction of the internees to the slaughter of people marching for their freedom on Bloody Sunday and the subsequent attempted cover up in the Widgery Report; the Abercorn Restaurant and the effects of the Provisional bombing campaign; the proroguing of Stormont; Aldershot and the shooting of John Taylor; the murder of Joe McCann; sectarianism; the effects of the violence on the economy; the possibility of civil war; violations of human rights. They have no rival for charting reaction within the internment camp to these events, or for an account of daily life for the internees and their relationships with the warders, the soldiers guarding them and the authorities running the internment regime.

The origins of the letters lie in a request to Des from a journalist with *The Irish Times* for a story from within Long Kesh. The first letters therefore address not so much the lives of the prisoners but the fact that the importation of warders from England at special rates of pay was causing friction between the warders and the authorities. The editor of *The Irish Times* and the doyen of twentieth-century Irish newspapers, Douglas Gageby, liked what he saw, and offered Des a regular slot in the paper, with copyright remaining with the author. Gageby was as good as his word, and every letter that was sent from Long Kesh appeared in the paper. The letters were handed over to Marie O'Hagan during her weekly visits to her husband, smuggled out by her, and from there sent down to *The Irish Times* for publication. They appeared around once a week, although there could be longer or shorter gaps in their appearance. The letters that appear here have had adjustments made for spelling and grammar errors, or for missing words, while the Irish has been modernised, and have had explanatory notes added. Other than these minor alterations, the letters appear as they did in 1972.

As already noted, the letters deal with a wide variety of issues, large and small, universal and very specific. What shines through them all, regardless of the theme, is the humanity of the author. We see him in playful and humorous mood when, for example, discussing the efforts of the internees to stave off the horrific prospect of a dry St. Patrick's Day. We see humour with a real edge, such as the barbs about how the experience of Long Kesh could benefit those seeking to build concentration camps in future. We also see him in a darker mood, the shock and horror of the events of Bloody Sunday silencing the men. Or when discussing the efforts of him and others to stave off depression as they watch others released. We can trace the fears of the internees as they watch the bombings and the sectarian killings causing further division, with the fear of civil war looming larger in their thoughts as time goes on. We see friendships forming, the internees trying to find ways to amuse themselves, the banter. The admiration for other prisoners trying to learn Irish, and the gratitude for those who write to the internees, send them books, or otherwise show solidarity. The families of the internees are not forgotten either, and there are reflections of the suffering of those left their liberty but deprived of husbands, fathers and sons. We even see empathy for the soldiers guarding him, and the hope that some common ground can be found. We also hear a lot about how cold it is in Long Kesh. The letters can make us laugh out loud, but we never forget that these are men deprived of their liberty without due process, and that this is a tragedy for them and their families.

On February 23, 1972, a letter to the editor appeared in *The Irish Times* from John Dillon of Portmarnock. 'I hope you are preserving the contributions of your Long Kesh correspondent, Des O'Hagan.'

He discerned in O'Hagan's writing 'the same masterly evocation of detail, the same human concern, and the same humorous eye in grim situations' as the very best writings from prison. Dillon concluded: 'At any rate, I would think that a collection of some kind of O'Hagan's prison journals would be one good thing that could be salvaged from Internment.'

These letters are being republished for the fortieth anniversary of the introduction of internment as a reminder of the damage that internment and the violation of civil rights by those in power did to our society. They also remind us of the need to defeat the sectarianism that has proved so damaging the to cause of progressive politics in Ireland. Still more, they remind us of our common humanity, of the power of ordinary people to challenge injustice, and of the need to educate and organise themselves to build a better society. Unfortunately, the warnings in the *Letters* about the need to heed Tone's call for the unity of Protestant, Catholic and Dissenter and the dangers of sectarian violence proved prophetic. However, the *Letters* display the optimism of the will that Gramsci judged essential to the revolutionary. They remain today what they were when they were first published: a rallying cry to the struggle to build a democratic, secular, socialist society on the island of Ireland.

DR ULTÁN GILLEN

Senior Lecturer in European (French) History
Teeside University

This book is dedicated to my late wife

Marie

who with no small degree of
courage and resourcefulness
smuggled the letters out of Long Kesh
each week for publication in
The Irish Times.

Further to the latter, I wish to acknowledge
the role of the paramount
Irish newspaper editor of his generation

Douglas Gageby
(Editor of *The Irish Times* 1963 – 1986)

who generously allowed me retain
copyright of the *Letters.*

Strike at Long Kesh of Prisoners and Warders - Dream of Solidarity

S OMEBODY, A DUBLINER FOR sure, calculated once that if everyone who claimed to have been in the G.P.O. in 1916 had been there then the G.P.O. would have had the dimensions of Croke Park. It is not that one wants to claim a similar history-making role for Long Kesh but I would not be surprised if the present population of 427 has not undergone the same process of multiplication in another thirty or forty years' time, unless the British Army makes exaggeration unnecessary.

Anyhow, there is no doubt about it. Long Kesh is gradually acquiring symbolic significance in the national consciousness.

No blasphemy is intended when I suggest that ex-residents will be held in the same awe as the annoyingly regular penitent at Lough Derg. Signs of the sacred, Mecca-like character of the spot have already manifested themselves. There has been a Christmas Day pilgrimage or almost one at any rate; senior secular holy men including the Leader of Her Majesty's Opposition at Westminster have come in search of self-knowledge and possibly public absolution. Big Ian did also and no doubt was genuinely hurt when he was denied the opportunity for heated discussion with Mad Mitch. (One has to admire Mitchell's bloody cheek.) A pity, as Ian knows what being inside is like and a chat with internees would have helped his image with Whitehall's Northern Ireland experts who must be desperately studying Mr. Faulkner's horoscope at the moment or whatever they do when change is imminent.

What the camp really lacks is a dedicated historian; maybe the Ford Foundation or Taca could help here. Somebody who would be able to state authoritatively at future meetings of the Irish Folklore Society what actually did happen.

In fact, the more I reflect on this idea and its national significance it becomes clearer and more urgent that a team of scholars should come here immediately. The historian should have the services of a sociologist, social psychologist, obviously a social anthropologist, ritual being the 'in' concept, a political scientist and if there is money to spare a theologian, what American academic institutions love to call a 'multi-disciplinary team.'

I did say immediately, as what now is fact could in six weeks' time appear to be fantasy.

For example, as is well known to criminologists, prisoners and their guards tend to form an in-group against threatening out-groups. The fairly quiet arrival of English prison officers has clearly set the scene for a unique industrial dispute along similar lines. I mean just about everyone here is threatened.

The local officers, who in the majority genuinely detest the sight of Long Kesh and are uneasy about their relationship with the British Army, are now working with what I suppose is best described as well-heeled scab labour.

Mr. Faulkner, unable, in spite of 10 per cent unemployment, to recruit warders locally has imported what one senior member of the prison staff has openly and colourfully described as a 'shower of effin English mercenaries.' Not only colourful but fairly accurate – there are two Gaelic-speaking Galwaymen and one Pakistani among the new arrivals – for they receive £12.50 tax free on top of the weekly flat rate.

In any other industrial situation, the reaction would probably be fairly prompt but the problem for the Irish prison officers is that they belong to the same union – association actually – as the English warders, which makes a difference. There are also some funny clauses relating to transfers, hardship allowances, official secrecy, shut-your-mouth-and-if-you-don't-like-it-you-know-what-to-do-Mac type clauses. All in all a fairly trying situation.

From the other side of the fence (sorry) there were bound to be reactions. There are serious Socialists here who believe in what are often just slogans. You know, solidarity with other workers, joint action, one out all out. Others naturally enough could not care less; a screw is just a screw.

There is also a national ingredient in the situation which

should not surprise anyone who has worked alongside an Orangeman in Birmingham. We are, after all, Irishmen in the face of the master race and if you find that hard to believe then your knowledge of Englishmen is derived solely from B.B.C. television. Still the issue is mainly industrial as there are Englishmen employed under local conditions: one distinguishes the foreigners by little polished buttons on the side of their caps.

It would be wrong to give the impression that the prison officers and the detainees are holding discussions with a view to a wage claim, work to rule or strike action. This could possibly happen with a Lenin in our midst but there is what I am sure Billy Craig* ould once have described as hard evidence of revolutionary activity. Tacit agreement has been reached between a number of internees and the local officers that the Isle of Wight visitors are to be told firmly that their presence in what is undoubtedly Ireland and our concentration camp is just not wanted. Even more forcefully, certain internees persist in reminding them that in the days of recruitment to the Palestine Police £50 all found was the sum mentioned in public advertising. The advertisement being amended to read, if I remember right, 'if you are found.'

The regular presence of a common enemy – one hopes that this is not some devilishly clever English plot to unite the Northern Irish at the most significant point of disagreement – is leading to a gradual erosion of the more

* William Craig, reactionary unionist politician, ex-Stormont Minister for Home Affairs responsible for the attack on the civil rights marchers at Duke Street on October 5th 1968. He formed the quasi-fascist Vanguard Movement in February 1972, encouraged loyalist paramilitaries, and threatened civil war and the liquidation of his enemies.

obviously authoritarian aspects of the camp and it is reliably reported that three warders were seen in the pouring rain kicking a ball about the central cage area when they are supposed to be on guard duty.

What I think future historians will judge to be dubious even though witnessed to here and now by this observer, is the fairly widespread feeling that there ought to be significant support from the internees in the event of industrial action by the prison officers. I fear that there will be no such action due to the nature of the warders' contracts. That this is tragic in the present distraught state of Northern Ireland will be clear to anyone who has been carefully following this piece of contemporary history. For a solution satisfactory to everyone from Miss Devlin to Mr. Heath seems to be contained in the following hypothetical headline:

Long Kesh Warders Strike –
Internees Come Out In Sympathy.

JANUARY 22ND 1972

A Blow Struck for Equality Within Internment Camp

THERE IS NO PRECEDENT, as far as I know, for the type of industrial battle which now seems to be on the cards in Long Kesh: unless, that is, one goes back to the few Glenravel Street police officers who in 1913 struck in sympathy with the Belfast carters. It is unlikely that Mr. Graham Shillington, RUC Chief Constable, will consider pulling his overworked men out of Palace Barracks* in solidarity with the increasingly disgruntled prison officers. Nor do I imagine, if the Irish Congress of Trade Unions decided to black the site, would the British Army refuse to ferry the daily requirements to the camp. Our efforts to encourage the soldiers to organise, educate and agitate have alas been received rather coldly. Their failure to understand the need for unionisation is a problem Jack Jones** might ponder on in this golden year of the T.G.W.U.

* Palace Barracks, Holywood, County Down was a notorious interrogation centre.
** At that time General Secretary of the Transport and General Workers Union.

This is not to say that the Irish warders have surrendered without a blow being struck for the honoured maxim of equal pay for equal work.

Part of their strategy, it seems, is to ensure that the most uncomfortable duty – none are onerous, all are boring – goes to the Englishmen. I do not want to sound too gleeful, but their present effort, making the best of frugal resources, is simply magnificent. Each cage exit is by way of two barbed wire gates and as internal security decrees that when one gate is open the other must be closed, one warder is engaged in a space of about nine square yards for nearly three hours at a time.

Undoubtedly the weather has helped, there having been quite a few soft Irish days recently, so that, of the original nine Isle of Wight volunteers, seven have returned to Parkhurst – a respectable decent sort of place apparently. They departed enthusiastic converts to Mr. Maudling's* view of this part of Ireland. One can see the tourist board lining up with those calling for Mr. Faulkner's head if the warders maintain their present success rate.

Mr. Faulkner is naturally enough regarded by one and all here with an intense identical emotion. Pollsters, psychologists, designers of questionnaires in general can be certain they would receive a 100% positive response about his responsibility for the present state of the community.

At the same time we follow his increasingly fewer

---

* Reginald Maulding, Edward Heath's Home Secretary: On boarding the airplane to leave Northern Ireland after his first visit, he famously remarked, "For God's sake, bring me a large scotch. What a bloody awful country!"

pronouncements closely, his recent interview on television being analysed, reviewed, dissected, studied and discussed from every possible angle. Not, I hasten to add, solely out of wishful thinking; the verdict was that he is a man on the brink. There is no point relating the catastrophes, natural or otherwise, which our collective genius could immediately provide if the Deity were to command our willing services. Suffice to say that the odds available here – we have our own bookie – would not lead to the placing of a single Woodbine in his favour. Our political experts, graduates cum laudae of the Curragh, Parkhurst, Derry, Crumlin, Mountjoy and Dartmoor, have voted him to be a 'baten docket.' As local racing men know, this refers to a losing bet: in Belfast clerks write each forecast for the punter, a touch of pre-bureaucratic warmth missing, I understand, from Southern betting shops. There are more serious matters dividing us than the modish two-nations theory would have it. Anyhow there is finality in the expression, an epigrammatic quality worthy of his last days at Stormont.

Clearly a single television performance would not provide all the evidence necessary for such dogmatism, yet even Mr. Faulkner's most ardent admirers, who may see in him something of the late President Kennedy or Pierre Trudeau*, could not but fail to be concerned by his appearance. Normally his facial expression is not one to inspire trust or confidence and it is regrettable that the question, 'would you buy a second-hand car from this man,' was employed so accurately elsewhere. But on this

---

* Pierre Trudeau was Prime Minister of Canada, and, like John Fitzgerald Kennedy, considered a charismatic and talented media performer.

occasion, Portadown matrons, had they read The Naked Lunch would have been convinced they were witnessing a junkie still suffering from a cold turkey cure for the habit. His worries certainly are legion: one doubts very much if even the kindly Captain O'Neill could have done his Churchillian thing at this time.

Our experts here, though, having more time than most to spend over the available entrails have been posing stimulating questions with regard to this particular programme. To be sure, Stormont does not provide much of an audience these days; but why exactly did Mr. Faulkner, clearly somewhat uneasy – even shifty – expose himself to what was for Irish television a uniquely rigorous interview? There was also an interesting fumbling intent to disclaim responsibility for the continuation of internment. That the programme went out from Havelock House, for some simply reflects Mr. Faulkner's pique with the other channels: there are others among us who in hunting for an eager pretender see in Mr. Bradford's* B.B.C. broadcast a subtle sign of willingness to wield the axe or administer the stab in the kidneys. Did his ultimate, apparently reluctant, admission that internment had resulted in massive alienation and polarisation within the community indicate a readiness to shoulder the cares of even an emasculated office and thus force Mr. Faulkner to plead for viewing time to tell once again about his repugnance for Long Kesh, the Maidstone, Magilligan and Crumlin.

There is a particularly nasty story circulating here that when the Prime Minister's office rang Ulster Television to

* Roy Bradford was the Stormont Minister of Development.

hastily arrange the details they were told by the programme director that the performer's fee would be the usual twenty-five guineas. Mr. Faulkner's cheque, it is said, was on his desk the following morning.

I am sure that this is not original but it does convey the general opinion of Mr. Faulkner.

You may be thinking that our time would be better spent on education, learning bridge or playing chess, than reading political teacups and there are a few who would probably agree with you. In fact, as someone put it only the other night, wading between the Nissan huts, 'we're only political prawns [sic] in the game'*. And on reflection there is a wealth of political understanding in that comment.

---

* This comment was made the late Mickey Brady of Leeson Street, Belfast

Early Morning
Visit from
an Army

S ECRETLY I USED TO count myself among those Irish
who suffer neither from ethnocentrism nor
Anglophobia, but, in spite of such sociological virtue, I
have succumbed to the certainty that the English middle
class are, in fact, an inferior breed. That effortless English
superiority which Rebecca West* revealed when
recounting an observation on William Joyce on
horseback, 'but he does not ride like a gentleman,' has
gone with the dignity, grace and charm of the empire.

Evidently there are still those who remain calm and
retain the proper values, as would be clear to anyone
reading the recent heated exchanges on the problems of
shipping polo ponies from Malta.

Stretched out on my bunk, in my inner eye I can see
the new English middle-class male stereotype. He is

* Rebecca West was the penname of the author Cicely Isabel Fairfield. The
William Joyce referred to is the US-born, Irish-raised Nazi propagandist Lord
Haw Haw, who was hanged in 1946 for his wartime radio broadcasts from
Germany.

identical with a Peter Sellers caricature of an Indian applicant for a responsible Government clerkship: in Cheam they smile indulgently at the nearly impeccable Oxbridge accent and the naive reliance on inferior qualifications (B.A. Bombay Academy (Failed)). What I am coming to - belatedly I admit - is the recent extravagant production - the great Long Kesh search. We have it on the most reliable authority (inside the War Office) that the Army's gin-and-tonic public relations officers - the accent is correct, the qualification nearly the same, M.A. Madison Avenue (Failed) - are now anxiously studying basic propaganda texts, the reading list having been strengthened to include the Compton Report on the advice of the more experienced MI5.

The black comedy began spontaneously at 4.30 a.m. Unencumbered by lack of planning, one thousand five hundred eager baying troops - we never saw a policeman - and selected breathless television crews hurried through hostile countryside to bleak, dank Long Kesh. Thoroughly briefed on arriving about the possible dangers, 20 soldiers sneaked into each hut, positioned themselves at the bedsides and waited.

Reveille is not normally the most urgent business of the day. There is little to attract one culinary-wise at any time but the truly icy cold interior of our living quarters makes surfacing a genuine act of will. Most of us are not easily startled, having arrived at Long Kesh via Girdwood or Holywood, but it is unusual to awaken at 6.20 to the gentle touch of the military, not dressed apparently for a riot.

'Good morning gentlemen' [sic] and we were then

informed that we must wait in bed until ordered to leave for the canteen: the great search had begun. Individually marched through a double rank of soldiers, supported by two attendants as the tarmac was slippery, one was poked by the gelly sniffer stuttering ominously in the corner of the canteen*. This dalek-like probe is unfortunately prone to vomit out condemnation at the most inoffensive of objects, nylon jackets literally causing it to gibber idiotically like a Stormont Minister confronted with the civil rights reform programme. The British Army's general lack of trust in advanced scientific procedures was neatly expressed by a disillusioned private that it would be easier to shoot the lot of 'em. Quite.

While the hunt continued one had glimpses of military-looking civilians sporting cameras and apparently enjoying what amounted to an inexpensive day at the races. One ebullient sergeant roughly modelled on John Wayne – the British Army increasingly appears like a branch of the Green Berets – suggested that music might help to dispel the gloom. Later it was regretted that no-one thought to call out 'Achtung, achtung, you will now listen to the music.' The Army is apparently aware of the need to counteract such a false image for one notices the flash of a gay scarf worn by an officer, encouraged possibly by the idiosyncratic styles and the ethos of the Battle of Britain. It would be more honest to accept Wayne.

One could sense that the 50 or so soldiers were bored, irritated, disenchanted with their role of threatening overseers in the packed Nissen hut. Some listened

---

* A device that searched for traces of gelignite. The unreliable science it was based on later helped wrongly convict the Birmingham Six.

interestedly to a discussion on the Pearce Commission*, significantly though as comparisons were made between themselves and the Todds, one intervened to state that they were there to do a job and do it they would: a potential political commissar. Dinner having been refused the hut suddenly rocked to *Óró 'Se Do Bheatha 'Bhaile*, followed by a spirited chanting of *The Boys of the Old Brigade*. Our songs betrayed varying understandings of the situation: what, I wonder, did these sons of Newcastle coalminers and Dorset farmers make of *Joe Hill*, *Connolly Was There*, *General Munro*, *Free the People*, *Rebel Heart*, *Larkin*, the *Belfast Brigade* and the *Internationale* in Gaelic? They tapped the rhythms, probably yearned for the familiar warmth of the noisy local. May they enjoy it soon.

Eight hours later they departed, according to reports elatedly displaying an esoteric range of diabolical instruments ranging from Stanley wood knives, dagger type darts – Jim Pike** should watch out – drills and a caveman's spoon. It may sound petulant, but had Army H.Q. requested these tools through the usual channels, then our visitors could have arrived as normally, we would not have been subject to maximum boredom, and valuable television time would have been saved. As a P.R. exercise it has appalled professional journalists who will now find it increasingly difficult to translate Army

* The Pearce Commission was appointed by the British government to examine public opinion in Rhodesia (now Zimbabwe) on plans that would give more black people the vote, but fell short of democratic majority rule. The former Prime Minister of Rhodesia, Garfield Todd, and his daughter Judith were arrested on January 18th 1972 due to their support for majority rule. Garfield Todd described his situation as imprisonment without trial.

** Jim Pike was a famous darts player of the 1930s and 1940s. He had an immensely popular type of dart named after him still used in 1972 handouts. Life is becoming impossible.

In an effort to help publicise Long Kesh and its struggling offspring, Magilligan, surely without wishing to sound didactic, one should emphasise the selling points of what is undoubtedly our only growing influence. Literally overnight Cage Six fully populated, functioning albeit imperfectly, has blossomed into life. Criticisms from ecologists, demographers and other doomsday theorists can be quickly dismissed as subversive, stemming from their covert sympathy for the reactionary Civil Rights movement. On the other hand, adroitly handled, such criticisms could be invaluable, being readily demolished by pointing out the successful nature of the experiment in terms of population relocation and new high densities: utilisation of formerly useless resources: reduction in unemployed: and a significant cutback in pollution. Having once made these points opposition from anti-internment organisations would collapse, all sensible, practical, informed and progressive opinion would swing to the Army.

Regular entertaining bulletins on the diverse qualities of the camp plus the occasional academic paper on its functional relationship to the economy would help project a balanced image. One could also employ redundant tourist officials conducting grand tours from H.M.S. Maidstone to Armagh, north to Magilligan, then to Crumlin Road, culminating at Long Kesh.

Our climate does not compare with Greece but we can offer superior facilities to natives and visitors alike.

Bleak Wake
for the
Derry Slaughtered

I T IS BITTERLY COLD here tonight. Sunday. We have been walking round the cage. Our breath puffs out and hangs momentarily in the sharp piercing air, the tarmac glitters darkly through a light down of snow, one can feel the hard mud ridges break underfoot and in between the cages frozen pools dully reflect the perimeter lights. Tonight is so clean, so pure that the distant sound of cars on the motorway seems like the rumble of the sea falling gently on the sand. The guard dogs bark quickly, then silence; one could be walking up through Gleann Finn enjoying the brilliant moonlight intent upon an evening's drinking and talking with good companions.

Sunday is newspapers, a surfeit of stories, columns of trivia, momentous accounts of world problems, dolly birds with ever briefer swimming trunks and swinging advertisements for swinging people. All the grossness of

Western civilisation is complied for our entertainment. I am not consumed by the puritan ethic but tonight this is my mood and I am sure the predominant emotion in Long Kesh.

Casually today we talked about Derry, in fact there had only been the occasional question about the march, forecasts of attendance were tossed out, someone may have raised the possible tactics of the Army. This was merely hours ago, now I forget. It is not that we were disinterested, we knew, quietly rejoiced that the people would assemble in their thousands on the heights of the Creggan, the women clutching at the weeuns' hands, the men muffled up against the winds blowing down the Foyle, looking stern as they stamped their feet, watching out for the famous. Many here have walked in the proud demonstrations, Coalisland, Enniskillen, Newry, Derry and Armagh. But now we are part of the marchers in a strange uneasy fashion. We should be there feeling the strength of the singing throng, hurrahing the slogans, jostling one another into louder voices and instead we are the objective. In this symbiotic relationship, separation is the consuming desire.

The first news of the monstrous actions came as some trouble in Derry. It was only to be expected, we said, Faulkner is intent upon demonstrating that he is as tough as old Brookeborough or any of the hardliners who bluster into Glengall Street and out of it advocating fire and brimstone solutions. Our interest waned slightly, to stop and talk means to feel one's feet freeze.

Then the first killings, two men had been shot – my mind jumped to Cusack and Beattie and last summer,

which is now so many deaths away. Derry is the Bogside
and Creggan: the square blocked Free Derry slogan
beckons one gaily from the old city announcing the vigour
of a hardened people. I have never been to Paris but I
imagine that I would find an arrondissement* having the
same harshness where the communards furiously erected
barricades, madly innocent of the deluge which would
overwhelm them. There is a quality, drawn from the Foyle
and sheltering Donegal, a colour in the people that must
be what the English mean when they boast about war-time
London. One feels romantically that it could happen here,
liberty, equality, fraternity might not be goddesses, but
works of human art.

The sombre nuance in the newsreader's voice quells the
angry shouts; we listen intently hearing incredulously the
increasing numbers of slain and wounded. Now
numbness invades the mind so that even the foulest
condemnations fall flat, lifeless on the hut floor. Bleak,
bleak is the night as we sit huddled ejaculating nonsense
to fill the void: we wake the slaughtered it seems,
automatically reverting to hushed tones as men conscious
of bereaved wives and coffins in the next room. One's
mind is dead but the senses quicken, other men's eyes
tighten, strain, surround the tears of pain, of sorrow and
stare harshly at their own souls.

We then stand behind the cameras watching the

* Paris is divided into administrative districts named *Arrondisements*. In 1871, in
the aftermath of the French defeat by the Prussians, the world's first working-
class revolutionary government emerged called the Paris Commune. The
Communards were viciously suppressed by a reactionary government based at
Versailles, with perhaps tens of thousands slaughtered when troops stormed
Paris

swollen streets, the Civil Rights banner raises a feeble cheer speedily quietened as the dragon water-cannon arcs across the screen. Often the sound of rubber bullets, the billowing gas, the slap of Army boots has sent our hearts thudding madly. Now we flinch at the squealing brakes, twist with the dodging youths: then the welling sickness – a sickness that will remain for days feeding on the horrors, the bitter vicious words, the images of crumpled bodies and a blood-soaked standard. The oaths sound hollow, feeble, useless; the men are dazed, groping for understanding as the twisted bodies disappear from view. The embittered face and repulsing flailing arm of one bearer epitomises all our emotions.

Tonight we do not sit late arguing the demerits of the E.E.C. or recalling the antics of old friends. I watch the quietness. In this crowded hut the isolation, the sudden fresh loneliness, is unbridgeable, bed is a sanctuary, sleep is coveted.

Tomorrow, or Tuesday: our gesture. It is our custom to honour the dead publicly, we stand facing inward, rows of silent men, hair catching the breezes, frozen faces, young and old. The roll of a drum leads the piper into the wailing keening 'Memory of the Dead', then the two minutes, hollowed-out peace. We scatter running for the huts, cursing the rain, the cold, the time, the camp, anything. To speak words always seems necessary as if the chatter here and now can erase the last few minutes. The Irish are, I am glad to think, embarrassed by displays of military glitter, our parades are more enthusiastic than disciplined, we do not goose-step or boast in hard satisfied tones of crack regiments and hard-hitting front-line troops. Our revolutionaries have been part-timers immersed more in living than in war. And this is right.

On this occasion we dip a Tricolour. It is camp made, nailed to a broom handle. Some will not even see it for the cages lie at angles cowering from each other. Close by every shoulder are the ghosts of the Bogside, but for our Derry comrades there is a special heartache, a grief we cannot share. One yearns for an eloquent Pearse at Rossa's grave or better still the passionate angry worker Connolly, a Northern voice, harsh, direct, demanding. From the cells of the Crumlin Road jail, one could see bulky Cave Hill, birthplace of the Republic; we have travelled about ten miles from there and the green and orange will remind some of us that no matter what distance others may have fled from the common name of Irishman that is what it is all about, why we are here is because at some time, somehow we believe that the men of no property will inherit this small part of the earth.

.

Security as Usual During Improvements

(or the case of the bookless library)

HE CELEBRATION OF THE first six months of internment (one sincerely hopes that this is not going to be a spectacular bi-annual event competing with Easter parades, the Twelfth and other illegal promenades) has prompted me to review the improvements in the amenities of Long Kesh; possibly also readers are interested in the ethos of the camp as I understand it, and this, I can categorically state, has not altered in any way.

Let me say at the outset that I now feel, as one of the reluctant pioneers of what I am afraid must be regarded as not an entirely successful project, a certain attachment – or rather a faint quickening of Behan's 'curious feeling' – for my present home.

On that account my judgments may tend to lack objectivity, but I hope that these proffered comments are not construed as simply malicious or vindictive. In a sense then, this is in the nature of a half-term report which could be of some use to future architects of similar schemes (though I would be the first to recommend that any tentative plans be scrapped and a less contentious form of public diversion be substituted). There is probably some demand for another Stormont, a minor royal residence or a new employment exchange.

It is in the nature of things where one day is remarkably like another that small changes should assume major dimensions. For example the decision by someone up there that boots should be provided for the internees is a welcome index that our dialogues with the camp bureaucrats actually do at times go beyond the barbed wire boundaries. Complaints, demands, requests are normally met by an intransigent negative, regularly described in the phrase 'for security reasons.' But the boots are more important in another, far more serious, sense because of the gigantic international plot revealed by Dr. Paisley some years ago, when he divined in the Civil Rights Association a conspiracy born from the Machiavellian marriage of Moscow and Rome. Dr. Paisley was as usual correct, as I discovered last week.

When I was forcing on what were described on the box as 'work laced boots, of leather, oil, benzene firm sole, made by *Grunit*', I was genuinely amazed to read the country of origin – the German Democratic Republic, here in Long Kesh, a Commie boot. It was almost like learning that Governor Wallace* had enlisted in the Black

* Governor George Wallace of Alabama was a notorious racist Democratic Party politician.

Panthers. My immediate reaction was not really on the conspiracy lines already mentioned, but rather one of righteous indignation that local-made footwear was not being used – Banbridge Chamber of Commerce should immediately raise this issue with Roy Bradford, our globe-trotting Minister of Commerce*. But as I waited on the cage gates being opened, the real truth suddenly dawned on my addled brain. The warder's numb fingers were having difficulty with the padlock and he naturally proceeded to blast the civil servant who had ordered inferior foreign locks.

There, stamped across the base in brazen letters, was 'Made in Italy.' The conclusion is patently obvious. The five hundred or so internees will be smuggled in the papish keys and, well shod in G.D.R. boots, will appear jovially leading a Civil Rights demonstration. Collapse of Stormont: the end of freedom, religion and laws.

Having mentioned security (which understandably is rather a touchy subject at the moment) I must add that the frustrations engendered by the word enrage most of the local staff as well as ourselves. In these circumstances it would be exceptionally difficult for a philosopher in the Wittgenstein tradition to maintain his belief in the aphorism 'the meaning of a word is its use.' In fact, I am not entirely unconvinced that the whole of modern linguistic philosophy may not have to be reworked in the light of our experience.

Security, it seems, is an infinitely elastic concept owning not even contestable boundaries. It is easy to appreciate that there will be a wide range of matters which

* Bradford was at the time Stormont Minister of Development, not Commerce.

will naturally fall under this heading, varying only according to the stringency of the criteria employed. A Hippie colony, one would imagine, would represent an extremity on a continuum, and Fort Knox the other. Long Kesh in this respect is definitely unlocateable. This is not, may I say, a recent phenomenon arising from the departure of one Francis McGuigan*, an event which, as far as I can gather, is not as yet entirely believed by the authorities. There is a haunted feeling, one detects, among the prison officers that he might suddenly reappear as magically as he departed. Rumour has it that if a certain local newspaper had not telephoned Stormont inquiring into an anonymous tip-off, his absence would, as yet, have remained unnoticed.

Some may be feeling that I am in the process of destroying my own case; the fact is that physical security was considered to be so satisfactory that none dared to contemplate even a single exception. Equally when the camp authorities are unable, unwilling, find it difficult to answer a question or are being bloody-minded they chorus 'security.'

There are literally fantastic examples of this non-rational, illogical behaviour. The bookless library (honestly) constitutes a prime example.

Long Kesh geographically embraces a number of separate cages, an administrative area, visiting block and a virgin all-weather playing field. There is doubt about the football field; some claim that it is, in fact, a heliport as 'copters land there regularly, while the goalposts, we are

---

* McGuigan became the first man to escape Long Kesh on February 7, 1972 by dressing as a priest and mingling with a group of visiting priests as they left.

reliably informed, are still being hand-carved elsewhere. At one end some months ago a large caravan was placed; this was to be our library, a prelude to a central education area proper. The prescient, Mr St. John Stevas*, had indeed informed a spellbound Westminster that library facilities were being improved. Although not short of reading material, thanks to our many friends, we patiently awaited the arrival of a stock of books: so far there is not even the faintest suggestion that the Ministry of Home Affairs are aware that Caxton** ever existed. Requests were then made that the caravan be made available as a study area, in particular for those preparing for examinations. In fairness it must be said that the bearer of ill-tidings blushed when he informed us that security demanded that the hut be surrounded by another wire fence before it could be used. Overshadowed by a gun-tower, surrounded by what would be six wire fences, clearly it is the Ministry's intention that when we have the opportunity to study that no-one will disturb us.

I had almost forgotten about my original intention to give an account of advances in conditions due to what I now see is an obsession with security: the disease is contagious. The problem is that as I write I am becoming increasingly conscious of the fact that this latest message may never find its way to Dublin so that if it does appear there can be general rejoicing at another breach in the fences. But there have definitely been improvements; of

* Norman St John-Stevas, Tory MP and one of a number of all-party MPs who visited Long Kesh in October 1971.

** William Caxton was the first person to introduce a printing press into England and was a major figure in the development of English-language publishing.

that I am certain. It is only a question of getting my mind off this other issue, security. It must be even more trying for Mr. Faulkner.

Beginning at the Beginning

S OME OF MY FRIENDS have been insinuating that I am not really writing about Long Kesh, that these occasional jottings fail to convey the claustrophobic, deadening, frustrating, hopeless, vicious, inhuman nature of the camp. (Is this better?) Fair enough, one good photograph or preferably a filmed documentary would be far more accurate in its portrayal of our daily existence. Indeed it is a pleasure to disclose that a brief 8mm. survey of Long Kesh produced by the camp council will soon be available; the film is in the can as far as I know and although not directed by Roman Polanski, it should make compulsive televiewing.

Anyway I have decided to accept the advice and accordingly begin at the beginning. Kesh as explained by Dineen's Irish-English dictionary has a variety of interesting meanings. I imagine that in the chthonian fastness of the Home Office when the problem of accommodating the growing number of political dissidents was being discussed and suitable housing debated, that a quiet unassuming expert - Problems, Ireland, North - pronounced in favour of the present site, his decision made not for security reasons, but from his deep passion for and long appreciation of Celtic themes and languages. Never having really been called on to advise on the plethora of difficulties besetting the province his career is at last justified: in one historic moment his years of careful study bore fruit and are crystallised in the apposite selection of the site - Long Kesh.

Personally speaking I stand in awe of *Ceas Uladh*. 'The periodic novena of languor to which Macha's curse subjected the Ulaidh.' Consider this in conjunction with a previous reference to the 'the pangs of labour': the absolutely Euclidean precision of the word plus these political, historical and social derivations alone must undoubtedly qualify it for the most startling, imaginative four-letter word ever. The emancipated mass media will soon be echoing to the sibilance of kesh this, that and the other. By then Mrs. Mary Whitehouse will be the leading activist of Women Against Internment and the final phase of the civil disobedience campaign begun with the devastating Clean Up Stormont, to which Mr. Faulkner will calmly reply 'Kesh off.'

Cis, ceis, ceis, ceas and ceas concentrate very satisfactorily every possible poetic nuance one would desire in a centre such as ours. The Language Freedom Movement might care to note this point as they hunt for initiatives: it could be that our failure, at this time, to understand Mr. Faulkner and his brand of Unionism is simply due to the compulsory use of Gaelic place names in the North: we might be more sympathetic to his public distaste for internment if we knew precisely where we were, in English that is.

I believe the generally accepted translation of kesh is a wattle fence and that there are a considerable number of places in the Down region bearing this title, which does not say much for the early Irish if they bore the slightest resemblance to this windswept plain. But I would rather strain a point to emphasise the other senses contained in Dineen. This, by the way, has the approval at least of our hut: linguists may be horrified but we arrive at most of our decisions in a thoroughly democratic way. There is general, ferocious agreement that a 'wicker basket' is an unexpected bonus which certainly could be applied to a prominent Keshian figure who alas in this instance must remain nameless*. Truly.

Dineen also is the accepted arbiter for the more serious activity of learning Gaelic; there are, in spite of the difficulties - space, din, no privacy - a large number of keen students. Culture, naturally, is a topic which provokes extreme attitudes, we still have advocates of the kilt as the definitive symbol of Gaeldom, while dismay at the downward plummeting of Man Utd would sadden Croke Park enthusiasts. Though I am inclined to think the ultimate statement on the question of the components of culture came from an Irish-Italian internee: on being harassed into taking up step dancing as a contribution to

---

* This is Robert Truesdale, the then Governor of Long Kesh.

the preservation of the national heritage he snorted: 'and if I plant potatoes I suppose I am supporting Gaelic agriculture.'

Being an Irishman still presents problems of definition, even in here; also the situation is not helped by the widespread canvassing of a two nations theory, which now not surprisingly appears to be official Conservative policy. There are one or two who accept it because it comes from the IC and BO* – others maybe because it seems to have the canonical blessing of the Roman Catholic Hierarchy (bigots). Dr. Cruise O'Brien's contribution is ignored as he is deemed an agent of Wilsonism: opponents range from simple souls who accept Tone and abhor sectarianism to an outraged sociologist who holds the floor occasionally at two a.m. swearing bitterly at what he describes as the sinister conspiratorial resurrection of medieval political concepts in neo-Weberian terms**. As most of us are in bed reading, sleeping or because we have learned his jargon (it sounds good) no-one bothers to question him. That is, until recently.

He had taken to prowling around alone the perimeter of our cage, which is definitely not his usual gregarious manner, muttering angrily about racism, sectarianism, socialist republics and religion. The storm broke a few days ago and we have been wallowing helplessly in the face of the profundity of his anti-holistic (but) functional theory of the new Ireland (his words). Under pressure he admits frankly that the analysis may have been floated

* A reference to the British and Irish Communist Organisation (BICO), which promoted the Two Nations Theory.

** This is a self-mocking reference by the author of himself.

elsewhere but that his primary purpose in presenting it now is due to status anxiety combined with the academic desire to be quoted as the source of the most-revolutionary theory since flower-power. We have excused him this last ambition as he assures us that the two nations exponents are themselves less worried about what they say, and more worried about who said it first, if you follow me.

His claims are absolutely outrageous. He proposes that Ireland become a loose federation of 32 autonomous county republics and in this fashion every possible problem will be solved. Unemployment, which like the poor we have always had with us, would be eradicated by the need for standing armies, smuggling, prime ministers, cardinals, moderators and secret agents. There could be secular societies, theocratic societies, communist societies, and there would of course be room for experimentation. Our tame sociologist further argued that provision would have to be made in the future for the different Protestant (and increasingly) Catholics brands of Christianity, as he says that no matter what one is born there is no guarantee what one will finish up. The citizens of the famous two nations theory will at that time be easily accommodated, he thinks, in places like Rathlin or Tory as real national criteria will have relocated them in the various republics.

He has also decided on the title of this exhaustive work (and awaits offers from interested publishers), which has a faint ecclesiastical tone, in order to preserve continuity with the original thesis: 'Pariochialism Rules'.

Revealed Depths of Incarceration

I WAS PLEASED TO READ last weekend that the British Army fire advisory service were expressing concern about the fire hazards to which internees were exposed in Long Kesh. There is touching kindness for you. But General Tuzo's consultants can rest easily as the possibility of a blaze here are remote. If one could picture a fire scudding across the frozen wastes of Alaska incinerating every last piece of ice then one has a fairly objective picture of the sort of raging inferno we might experience.

A one-line passage in the alleged report claimed that the Army's responsibility ended at the wire. This is also very gratifying though it should cause serious concern to the security section about the identities of the 50 or so soldiers who appeared in our cage on Saturday evening last. As a prelude to the arrival of men from Magilligan and the Maidstone some shuffling in personnel between cages was undertaken. We were marshalled, backs to the fences, facing a tight half-circle of baton-tapping troops.

The horrifying appearance of a modern soldier is to my mind one of functional concentrated menace. They have learned the importance of projecting the correct image: the slow rise and fall of a baton into a caressing palm which emphasises the blunt sickening thickness of its skull smashing end can loosen the springs of fear in the toughest hearts. It is equally terrifying to know that these are young working class men eager for their first bloodletting. Yet occasionally, and more so of late, privates whisper their distaste for their concentration camp duties, their desire to get away from our enraged women and children whose frenzied defence of their homes they can appreciate and understand. Members of the famous Gloucesters Regiment have complained bitterly about their brutal role in Belfast.

Our knowledge of the outside world, the real world of Ballymurphy, the Falls, Turf Lodge, Divis Flats, comes to us through returned parolees, in the main temporarily freed to attend funerals. Personal anguish has not touched me in Long Kesh, the consuming grief that is unknowable to others, but death has visited here so often that now there are men here who stare into the dark with only morning to come.

Who can say that the imminent death of a spouse whispered by a warder, suddenly in the night, is not a tragedy so great as to be indescribable? (She was buried on the morning of the explosion at the Parachute H.Q. in Aldershot). We know the helpless, huddled streets dipping off the Falls which fill with the threatening bulk of armoured cars: doors crash in as shouted orders send hearts thumping madly: women who daily must face the soldiers' taunts, the jeers, boldly stare down young eyes, wake startled, wild in the night. Such acts threaten the not so young: death then stalks Long Kesh. Our condolences must sound stereotypes for we have had much practice. We cannot diminish the grief of friends who lose wives, sons, brothers, their sorrow attracts no messages from those in secular or sacred office. Yet that man's emptiness is poured into this void so that we brush shoulders with infinite pain and hastily avoid eyes which hold loved images laced with barbed wire ribbons.

When one catches brief glimpses of children's faces twisted, not with tears, clutching desperately at their fathers' shoulders, the nightmare corridor between the visiting boxes becomes a spur to unreasoning anger. It is then, also, that one realises the awful dimensions of each man's incarceration.

In some senses there are unique personal insights to be gained from imprisonment. To have read Wilde's De Profundis or The Ballad of Reading Gaol in the cold womb of a prison cell can be to be confronted with, as Seosamh Mac Grianna, once said, the dark side of one's own soul*. I do not think I really understood that until now, understanding that in one's own mortality is brutality born. This realisation does not bring with it the end of dread, a quietening of nerves full stretched but rather it sharpens the points of senses so that this instant can be held almost pleasurably. On first seeing the

---

* A reference to Oscar Wilde, who was jailed as a result of his homosexuality. Seosamh Mac Grianna was an Irish-language writer from Donegal who had fought in the Black and Tan War and was interned by the Free State during the Civil War. He suffered from severe depression, living much of his life in a psychiatric hospital.

revelation that 'the most terrible thing about prison life is not that it breaks one's heart, for hearts were made to be broken, but that it turns one's heart to stone' (De Profundis), I thought, that is true. Now it feels wrong and I hope that this is not self-deception, for although we are deprived of many things one is still aware of dismay, love, fear, anger, distrust, hate. But possibly Wilde was consumed with such a fierce emotion that he felt no heat.

There is to my mind a warmth of spirit which is a necessary part of being human; it can lead to appalling acts and those who commit them know and regret it. Their instant terrifying nature feeds the appetite of a public weaned on headlines that dull the senses to the more lasting horrors. Instant judgments, public announcements follow, aimed at a desired end irrespective of events; demons and demi-gods are created, dangerous myths which should not be permitted to surface from our pre-history: meaning is eroded, language is debased by embodied Delphic voices who for too long have been deaf to the screams of the suffering.

Naturally I am writing of the tragedies of Aldershot and the attempted assassination of John Taylor, Minister of State for Home Affairs at Stormont*. To be honest, they have not provoked the same concern or reaction expressed in various parliamentary announcements and questions. Our vision is probably distorted, our judgment

---

* On February 22, 1972, the IRA bombed the Parachute Regiment's headquarters in retaliation for Bloody Sunday, destroying the officers' mess. The seven people killed were a British Army chaplain, a gardener and five female cleaners. The next day, the IRA apologised for the civilian deaths. The IRA also shot John Taylor on 25th February on the grounds that he was partly responsible for Bloody Sunday.

warped, so that we cannot appreciate what we are told by our Westminster overlords who display such concern for law and justice. We have heard Sir Alec Douglas-Home's lofty defence of the Smith Regime's imposition of law and order on Rhodesian Africans and listened in silence to Heath's condemnation of the picketing techniques of unruly miners: we have not even been moved by either of their humane speeches. In our long discussions it is unlikely that anyone understood or agreed with the political concepts employed by these non-violent men.

To be sure there may be some here who rejoice in violence in the same way as I believe that Pearse or Fanon did. This is their burden. For the vast majority violence has meant sectarianism, the degradation of the dole queue, slum houses, poverty, educational rejection and of recent years the repression of the ghettos by the British Army. Yet all are saddened by the death of any civilian: we do not send to see for whom the bell tolls.

Each day, each night we live in this violent deprivation of our freedom which I am afraid will take its mental and physical toll. (One man has been quietly released through a mental hospital recently). I am not attempting in writing this or in my earlier comments to provoke arguments around Old Testament criteria for justice: such would be sterile. But in as much as the men of Long Kesh are for so many the heart of the present agonising destructive situation it is surely worth saying that for us, as far as we can learn, the awful guilt for every death must be borne by those who seem to balance parliamentary votes against a search for justice.

.

Efforts to Combat Deprivation on the National Day

ST PATRICK'S DAY IS looming threateningly arid on the horizon. Alcoholics Anonymous and the Pioneers of Total Abstinence, probably secret advocates of internment, can be imagined gloating over the prolonged decline in the sales of the diet of Northern drinking men, a bottle and a half 'un. (Some of us have friends who drink obscene imperialist beverages with an international reputation. It is interesting that they remain free: virtue indeed must have its own reward.) Strenuous efforts are now being made to combat this deprivation which is assuming a truly poignant form as the national day approaches. My father, who could not sing to keep himself warm, used to chant monotonously:

The rain poured down as we flocked into town with our flags and our green banners waving. The band it did play God Save Ireland on St. Patrick's Day.

We will have a parade but it will lack the sort of colour,

promise, thirsty impatience to break the ranks which I am sure the Hibernians always displayed.

Our drink engineers, brew chemists, have had a fair degree of success in the past, although the after effects, as far as I am concerned, were sufficiently devastating not to encourage me to try again. It felt more like food poisoning than a hangover. On the night in question following lock-up at ten o'clock, we supped steadily, yarning, singing the favourites – the chorus of *Rann na Feirsde* is very popular on occasions like that – it was only when the time for solo renderings arrived that it was clear that some of us were definitely well on. It is reasonably fair to assume that if the *Birth of the Blues* is belted out half a dozen times in succession the singer is not sober; in my own case, being normally aware that I am father's son singingwise, our hut was shattered, silenced, sobered by the weird howling of *Faith of Our Fathers*.

Our first feis, or rather feiseanna, as each cage is unfortunately autonomous, will include the normal range of activities with special attention devoted to the internment skills: plaques, crosses, musical boxes, dolls' houses, decorated hankerchiefs, both commemorative and predictive will be judged. For the physically active, footraces around the cage perimeters are being arranged, the winner of the Long Kesh mile should receive, in my opinion, a special reward for his ability to speed round a circumference which would normally leave one prostrate with dizziness. As we are plagued with mice clattering across the corrugated iron hut roofs we are also trying to organise a hunt led by the cage cat 'Freedom' and the few poachers in our midst. Mr. Craig, who is something of a

Pied Piper, would be very welcome at the moment.

Fifth Avenue's jaunt will undoubtedly be watched by thousands more puzzled onlookers as the Irish-Americans stride for freedom and justice, but it will be easier explaining our shenanigans to a handful of English warders than trying to tell New York's minorities why the day's festivities are dulled by black armbands. Harlem's Negroes would be better hearing about Ireland and Derry from Angela Davis than Judge Comerford*.

Like many other people who are gradually losing interest in the subtle non-answers of politicians – in fact I believe that some of the occupants of another cage have been consulting the occult via an ouija board in the hope of learning the content of Mr. Heath's cliff-hanging initiatives. The spirits consulted had not even pure speculation to offer. What genuinely amazes us is not the sickening speed with which new legislation can be passed at Westminster when Britannia's robes seem about to trip her up, but that all sorts of circumlocutions, pauses, shady deals, seem to be necessary, even in the eyes of one's friends, when the internment issue in discussed. Anyhow, both Connolly and Pearse – who else would they consult – kept their other-wordly information and were equally reluctant to give partisan support to any of the present

* Angela Davis was a member of the Communist Party of the USA who also had links with the Black Panthers. Ronald Reagan ensured that she lost her job at the University of California, Los Angeles due to her politics. In August 1970, guns she had bought were used in a hostage taking and escape attempt during which a judge, prosecutor, juror and three black defendants were shot dead when police opened fire. Davis ended up on the FBI's Most Wanted List. She was acquitted by a jury. Judge James J. Comerford was a veteran of the Black and Tan War who had emigrated to America. He was a conservative nationalist who chaired the New York St Patrick's Day Parade Committee.

political parties.

There are many shades of opinion contained here in spite of Mr. Faulkner's clever portrayal of internees as identical in character and outlook. All, however, were nauseated as the horror stories of the Abercorn Restaurant* were related; condemnation of what was a gross terrorist act was total and unequivocal. Men whose stories of personal suffering are in themselves shocking could hardly find words to express their abhorrence of the maniacs who had so callously murdered and maimed innocent people. Now there is depression, a lethargy has gripped us. How extensive it is would be impossible to say, although it appears to have affected not only those who are politically aware but the many who found themselves galvanised into active resistance against sectarian mobs who seemed about to swamp their homes in August 1969, and on that account, as a threat to the community, have been interned. I do not want to convey any sense of superior or inferior, for surely it is an excellent thing to wish to defend one's family, one's friends, from the ravages of organised swarms of bigots. The difference is that a genuine human emotion has evolved into the counterpart of what it sought to oppose; this distinguishing it from the ongoing secular, socialist tradition of republicanism. It is as if one had suddenly become aware of fear, fear not only for oneself but for the entire community.

Last July, off the Shankill Road, an area of slum

---

* On March 4, 1972, the indiscriminate Provisional bombing campaign struck the Abercorn Restaurant in Belfast. Two people were killed and over one hundred and thirty injured – many of the injured losing limbs. The attack so horrified public opinion that the Provisionals refused to claim responsibility.

housing so much like the Falls, I remember talking to people about the ridiculous Belfast Corporation plans for urban renewal, tower blocks of flats which would kill the local communities. I was there in the company of members of the *Seven Days* team who were preparing a background programme on the Twelfth. (Ironically the researcher is now in trouble with the R.T.É. establishment.) We were received courteously, the only complaint heard was the indifference of the Northern mass media to human living conditions. All that seems so far away, separated by a contrived chasm of blood and violence.

To have been in Long Kesh will now mean, for many of the working class, to be blood tainted – it is hard for people to distinguish shades of opinion, faced with Weatherman-type violence*. When reasonable men like Mr. Robb, surgeon at Belfast's Royal Victoria Hospital, find it hard to look at the future then it is slightly ridiculous to pose the question as to what reception Oliver Donohue and myself would have on the Shankill Road now.

---

* The Weathermen were a left-wing group who engaged in a bombing campaign in the USA.

Meanma
an
Champa

T Á CAMPA GÉIBHINN NA Ceise Fada lán anois ó chúl
go doras. Déarfainn go bhfuil chóir a bheith 700 fear
anseo faoi láthair agus ar feadh m'eolais tuilleadh bothán
á dtógáil ag na húdaráis ar a seacht ndícheall. Ar fad,
ceapaim go mbeidh deich gclós ann: is ionann sin agus
spás do míle braighdeanach. Má leanann seo ar aghaidh
ní fada go mbeidh an campa ar imeall Bhaile Átha Cliath.
Ní gá don Loingseach* ach cur leis an Cheis Fhada go
rúnda ansin agus beidh gach fadhb réitithe.

Duine ar bith a chaith seal i mbraighdeanas sa
Churrach beidh sé a dhéanamh gur saineolaí é ar
champaí, ach m'fhocal chuirfeadh an áit chaidheach seo
iontas an domhain air. I mbothán s'agamsa tá Éamann Ó
Cianáin a bhí i gcuideachta Mháirtín Uí Chadhain ansin
sna daicheadaí agus taobh liom Liam Seán Mac Corraidh
a bhfuil an dubhrud scéalta aige faoin Mháirtín chéanna.
Diabhal falsa amach is amach ab ea é de réir Liam. Ní

* An Taoiseach Jack Lynch.

nífeadh sé a chuid éadaí ach uair sa ráithe agus b'ait ar fad an dóigh a rachadh sé ina gceann. Chuirfeadh sé na héadaí ina gcnap mór i mbairille uisce the, cúpla paicéad púdair istigh ar a mbarr, ansin ar shiúl leis fá ghnoithe éigin níos tábhachtaí. Thiocfadh sé ar ais i gceann cúpla lá leis an uisce a athnuachaint. Lá nó dhó eile agus chrochfaí na héadaí glana ar líne. Tá scéal eile ag Liam ach ní féidir a aithris anseo, is trua. Cibé ar bith é, deir siad liom go ngoilleann an tréimhse seo imtheorannaithe míle uair níos measa orthu ná na blianta fada ar mhachairí Chill Dara. Ceart go leor, aithním go bhfuil siad níos aosta anois ach creidim iad.

Is é an rud is spéisiúla ó thaobh Gael de a laghad cainteoirí Gaeilge atá inár measc. Ní dóigh liom go bhfuil níos mó ná baicle beag ann ar fad, iad scaipthe fríd an champa. Agus níl macasamhail Mháirtín linn ar chor ar bith, faraor. Den aicme oibre bunús na bhfear ach is beag suim a chuireann a bhformhór i scríbhinní na réabhlóidí a chothaíonn an t-aicmeachas, seachas an mhuintir a dtugtar Poblachtánaigh Oifigiúla orthu. Labhair mé le hArt Mac Maoláin, Cathaoirleach Chomhchoiste na gCumann Poblachtánach ar caidé a bhí na cumainn a dhéanamh i dtaca le hoideachas de. 'Tar éis Lá 'le Pádraig,' a dúirt sé liom, 'beidh scoil seachtain iomlán againn i gclós a cúig: léachtanna gach tráthnóna ar ábhair mar shóisialachas, poblachtánachas an Chómhargaidh; istoíche sna botháin pléifear na ceisteanna achrannacha i ngrúpa. Tá muid ag súil go mbeidh muid ábalta cúpla paimfléad a fhoilsiú ar na díospóireachtaí.' Chaith sé féin breis is ceithre bliana sa Chromghlinn ag deireadh na gcaogaidí. Aontaíonn sé gur measa i bhfad an t-achar seo

sa Cheis Fhada ná blianta sa phríosún. In aon bhothán le
hArt cónaíonn Proinsias mór Mac Giolla Eid ('Fear
Maith'). Seo an tríú huair aige bheith faoi ghlas mar
bhraighdeanach. Gabhadh é sa Deisceart le linn na
dtrioblóidí deireanacha.

Ní hé an duine is sine é ar an champa gidh go bhfuil sé
ag tarraingt ar an trí scór bliain. Níl a fhios agam faoi
Dhia caidé mar is féidir le Faulkner gunnadóir a thabhairt
ar a leithéid d'fhear. Ceart go leor is Poblachtánach go
smior é; ní dóiche go bhfuil aon fhear sa tír níos díograisí
d'fhíorchúis na Poblachta ná é, ach measaim gur fuath
lucht an Special Branch ar a chalmacht a chuir isteach
anseo é. Is cuimhin liom le linn dúinn bheith in
Girwood é ina shuí ar an urlár. Bhí thart fá chéad againn
ann agus slua mór saighdiúirí ag siúl thart ag bagairt
orainn. Mhothaigh mé Proinsias a dhul don phóilín airm
seo as rud éigin a dúirt sé - char chuala mé i gceart caidé a
bhí á rá aige - ach d'imigh mo dhuine mar pháiste a fuair
léab teanga óna mháthair. Is beag duine a rinne gearán le
fórsaí na Breataine na laethe sin, tá mé ag inse daoibh.
Eisean duine de na daoine a choinnigh lasair na Gaeilge
beo ag daoine coitiantachta sa Tuaisceart nuair ba
shuaitheantas meánaicmeach í ag cléir agus múinteoirí
scoile. Níor dhearmad sé riamh gurb ionann
Poblachtánachas agus saoirse na haicme oibre.

Béal Feirstigh is mó, dar ndóigh, a tógadh agus cinnte
má tá clú agus cáil ar dhuine ar bith is beag nár chuala
trácht ar Shéamus Ó Súilleabháin, nó mar a thugtar air
abhus 'an Tiarna Leeson'. Nuair a scríobhfar stair na
linne seo ó 1969 ar aghaidh aithneofar an pháirt mhór a
d'imir sé, thar aon duine, ag tógáil na gcoistí sráide, ag

eagrú an phobail, a d'fhulaing ionsaithe marfacha an
RUC agus ag bunadh an CCDC*. Ar na mallaibh
thoisigh sé ar stair na heagraíochta a scríobh. Ceardaí
adhmaid é Séamus, na huirlisí istigh anseo leis, mar sin de
ní stadann sé de bheith a shíorghearradh croiseanna,
plaiceanna, chuile sheort i gcomhair an fheachtas
bolscaireachta atá á reáchtáil faoi Chomhairle an
Champa. Cheap saighdiúirí Séamus i lár Bhéal Feirste, é
ar a bhealach go teach slán i gcomhair na hoíche. Ó tharla
blagaid air bhí sé a chaitheamh fuig mar bhréagriocht agus
ní ligfidh na daoine óga dó dearmad a dhéanamh gur thit
sé de nuair a bhí sé ag teitheadh ó na Fórsaí. Déanta na
fírinne, dóbair dó éalú an oíche chéanna.

Fear eile nach bhfeicim ach go fíor-annamh, de
thairbhe déantús na háite seo, é Malacaí Mac Biornaigh a
raibh an mí-ádh air nuair a thug na póilíní ruaig ar Bhaile
Uí Mhurchú. Tharla an lá fá dheireadh muid a chaint ar
dhrochíde, ghríosáil, bharbaracht Holywood agus na
cleasanna frithdhaonna a cleachtaíodh ansin. Is maith atá
a fhios ag pobal Bhéal Feirste nach féidir bheith ag súil
ach le brúidiúlacht ó Fhórsaí Cosanta na Breataine, ach
chuir scéal Mhalacaí déistin orm. Baineadh a chos ina
hiomláine de agus é ina thachrán buachalla. Anois tá cos
crainn faoi. Cuireadh ina sheasamh in éadan balla é;
ansin tugadh cic ar an chos go dtitfeadh sé ar a aghaidh.
Ina luí dó, sheas póilín ar a chnámh droma go ndeachaigh
sé i laige. Mhúscail sé san otharlann, é cinnte go raibh sé
ag cailleadh a stuaime. Le linn na dtrí lá a chaith sé i
lámha cineálta na bpóilíní chonaic sé beirt dochtúirí, nó
daoine a cheap sé a bheith ina ndochtúirí - Mac Gréagóir,

* Central Citizens Defence Committee, Béal Feirste.

Ó Murchú. Ní hamháin nár éist siad leis na raon gearán fán íde a fuair sé ach rinne siad magadh faoi, a dhearbhú go raibh cuma níos folláine air a dhul amach dó ná mar a bhí ar theacht isteach dó. I rith an ama dhiúltaigh sé aon chaitheamh ná deoch seachas uisce a ól ar eagla go raibh sé drugáilte acu. Ba chiallmhar dó é, mar fiú amháin nuair a caitheadh isteach i bpluchóg sa Chroimghlinn é d'fhéadfadh sé na tormáin agus an screadach a chluinstin go fóill.

Ní labhraíonn sé ar dhíoltas nó is Sóisialach Poblachtánach ó íochtar Bhóthar na bhFál é a d'obair go díograiseach in éadan na bpolasaithe diúltacha frith-Phrotastúnacha atá á scaipeadh go forleathan sa Tuaisceart anois. Chítear dó nach bhfuil ach todhchaí amháin i ndán dúinn abhus. Muna stadfar den phléascadh agus den anscrios, sin cogadh uafásach idir na Caitlicigh Rómhánacha agus na Protastúnaigh. An toradh a bheas ar an tragóid sin ná críochdheighilt úrnua (ar dhul na Cipire) sa Tuaisceart, ina bharúil. 'Amach anseo caithfear a shoiléiriú don phobal cé is ciontach as an staid ina bhfuil muid i láthair na huaire - níos faide siar ná mar a bhí sular thoisigh Cumann Ceart Sibhialta an Tuaiscirt,' a dúirt sé. Ach sin scéal nach bhfuil fairsingeacht ann dó anseo.

Bunaíodh craobh den Chumann Ceart sa phríosún sular bogadh muid go dtí an Cheis Fhada. Ag an am sin bhí Séamus Ó Tuathail agus Caoimhín Mac Gorraidh linn. Ó shin i leith tháinig níos mó ball isteach. Anois tá breis agus céad ar fad sna clósanna éagsúla, ina measc siúd Dennis Cassin ó Ard Mhacha a thaistil na Stáit Aontaithe a bhailiú airgid, a scaipeadh eolais ar dhrochstaid mhuintir an Tuaiscirt. Atoghadh é mar bhall de Ard-Choiste CCST ar na mallaibh ag an chruinniú chinn bhliana. Dar leis, tar éis Iúr Cinn Trá, go bhfuil formhór na ndaoine sásta glacadh le treorú an Ard-Choiste sin.

'Sóisialachas an t-aon leigheas ar fhadhbanna na tíre,' a deir sé, 'agus níl mé a mhaíomh rud ar bith eile seachas seilbh iomlán ag an aicme oibre ar mhaoin iomlán na tíre seo.

'Tá barraíocht cainte na laethe seo fán áit atá ag rachmasaithe i saol geilleagrach na tíre, daoine a stealladh ráiméise fá shóisialachas Críostaí. Is éigin don aicme oibre cumhacht a ghabháil daofa féin. Ciallaíonn sé sin réabhlóid iomlán i saol na hÉireann agus níl ach dream amháin atá lán-dáiríre fá dtaobh de seo. Fágaim fút féin cé hiadsan.'

Scríobhann Dennis chuig an-chuid daoine ag iarraidh a léirmheasa ar chúrsaí polaitíochta a nochtadh fríd an fhuath atá ag méadú gach lá dá dtig. I ndeireadh dála ceapann sé go dtiocfaidh na hOibrithe chun na tuigbheála céanna agus atá aige féin.

Leanfar de amárach . . .

. . . ar lean ó inné

T HÁINIG MUID ANSEO CHÓIR a bheith sé mhí ó shin. I dtús báire cha raibh ach dhá chlós. Ó shin mhéadaigh líon an champa fá chúig, beagnach. Is furasta a shamhlú go mbíonn deacrachtaí le réiteach: ráitis le cur amach ag nochtadh intinn na bhfear ar na cúrsaí a mbaineann leo agus an bun-iarratas sinne a scaoileadh saor. Socraíonn an Chomhairle an seort seo polasaí don champa. Bhí troid chrua leis na húdaráis lena chinntiú go mbeadh coiste den chineál seo ann a d'fhéadfadh labhairt go húdarásach leis an domhan mór. D'éirigh linn agus tagann na hionadaithe le chéile trí huaire in aghaidh na seachtaine le cúrsaí a phlé.

Ag amharc siar anois is doiligh a fheiceáil gur beag athrú a tháinig as an dian-obair a chuir baill na Comhairle isteach. Níl an fhaiche imeartha réidh; tá muid gan leabharlann, ach ag an am céanna is cinnte gur chuir muid go mór leis na fir fanacht aontaithe in éadan córas céasta na gclósanna. Chomh maith leis sin nuair a éiríonn achrann idir sinne agus an gobharnóir, thig leis an champa gníomhú mar aon fhear. Ar na mallaibh b'éigean do na húdaráis cúlú ó ordú a thug siad go gcaithfeadh na

fir a gcuid bróg a bhaint daofa sula ligfí ar cuairt iad.
Diúltaíodh dó seo. Anois ar an taobh amuigh b'fhéidir go
gceapann sibh gur rud suarach é seo. Is iad na cuairteanna
an chuid is tábhachtaí i saol na bhfear. Dá gcluinfeadh
sibh an gháir a chuaigh suas nuair a fógraíodh gur linn an
lá thuigfeadh sibh i gceart é.

Tá an Chomhairle bunaithe go daonlathach ar vótaí na
bhfear gan aon tagairt do na heagraíochtaí atá beo
beathaíoch istigh anseo. Ar an dóigh sin is féidir a rá go
hionraic go labhraíonn an coiste ar son tromlach na
mbraighdeanach. Dár ndóigh, tá siad ann nach bhfuil
sásta ach is beag an méid iad. Nuair a tháinig muid i
gcionn a chéile den chéad uair ceapadh Seán Ó Cianáin
as Doire Cholm Cille ina chathaoirleach agus Pádraig S
Mac Giolla Éin mar rúnaí. Toghtar an cathaoirleach. Is é
Séamus Ó Droma (Béal Feirste) atá sa phost anois.

Seo an darna huair faoi ghlas ag Padaí mar go leor leor
eile, ach is iontach ar fad an dóigh ar chaith sé é féin
isteach san obair rúnaíochta ag gríosáil daoine le troid in
éadan an chórais, ag brú ar an choiste bheith a
shíorsmaointiú ar dhóigheanna agus bheartanna nua le
ceist an imtheorannaithe a choinneáil os comhair an
tsaoil. Ag an am céanna troideann sé go pearsanta níos
fearr ná aon duine eile ar an champa. Ar na mallaibh
chuir sé an dlí ar an Tiarna Carrington as ucht roinnt
abairtí a dúirt sé fá na braighdeanaigh uile bheith ina
ndúnmharfóirí agus gunnadóirí. Tá muid ag fanacht go
mífhoighdeach le toradh an cháis seo.

Déarfainn go bhfuil cás maith eile aige mar eisean
duine de na daoine a tugadh ar shiúl ar an 9ú Lúnasa,
1971 go gcionn seachtaine. Bhí mé ag caint leis agus na

fir eile díreach i ndiaidh daofa theacht isteach sa phríosún
- bhí a shliocht orthu. Ba é Séamus Ó Tuathail i gcomhar
le Padaí a rinne sár-obair an t-am sin ag tabhairt ar
dhaoine ráitis a scríobh ag cur síos go cruinn ar chuile rud
a tharla le linn daofa bheith i lámha na bpóilíní airm. Tá
mé féin daingean cinnte muna ndéanfaí sin ag an am sin
gan sos gan staonadh nach gcluinfeadh aon duine faic fán
bhrúidiúlacht mhídhaonna a cleachtaíodh in Girdwood
agus Holywood. Tá míle buíochas ó gach braighdeanach a
dhul leis an bheirt acu as an scéal a chur ós ard.

Is le linn do Sheán Ó Cianáin a bheith ina
chathaoirleach gur toisíodh ar fheachtas bolscaireachta le
cuidiú leis na hiarrachtaí a bhí á ndéanamh ar an taobh
amuigh. Fear eile é Seán a bhfuil an-taithí ar an
phríosúnacht aige. Ní gearr go bhfaca sé an tábhacht a bhí
leis an scéal fá dhálaí an champa a scaipeadh go
forleathan. Chuaigh muid beirt, ar leithscéal fá
scrúduithe Gaeilge, thart ar na clósanna go léir a mhíniú
an phlean agus a thaispeáint do na fir nach raibh siad
cloíte cionn is iad a bheith i ngéibheann. Taobh istigh de
choicís scríobhadh níos mó ná míle litir, dathaíodh an
méid céanna ciarsúr, gearradh roinnt céadta plaiceanna.
Ós íseal a rinneadh an obair agus ós íseal a chuaigh na
hearraí déanta amach. Fosta, bunaíodh
'Comhchomrádaithe na Ceise Fada', eagraíocht do
dhaoine ar mhian leo cur in éadan an imtheorannaithe.
Anois bíonn teagmháil phearsanta ag na fir leis na céadta
daoine fríd an domhan, daoine a scaipeann go
leitheadach nuacht ón champa. Ní féidir a mheas go fóill
cén toradh a bheas ar an síolchur seo, ach tagann litreacha
ó chóir a bheith chuile chearn den domhan, fiú amháin

an tSeapáin. Caithfidh sé go bhfuil Seán Ó Dí* rud beag buartha fán fheachtas.

Ó d'éirigh Seán Ó Cianáin as an phost is le neartú craobhacha Chonradh na Gaeilge a chaitheann sé bunús a chuid ama: é féin agus Seán Mac Eachaidh is cúis le cibé suim a chuireann na daoine óga i bhfoghlaim na teanga. (Sula ndéanfaidh mé dearmad ba mhaith liom, thar ceann na nGaeilgeoirí, fíorbhuíochas a ghabháil le muintir Inniu, Amárach, Gael-Linn, Conradh na Gaeilge, Comhaltas Uladh as leabharthaí, ceirníní agus nuachtáin a sheoladh chugainn. Cuidíonn sé go mór linn fios a bheith againn go bhfuil spéis ag na heagraíochtaí náisiúnta Gaelacha ionainn). Mar chuid d'imeachtaí Lá 'le Pádraig is rún don choiste ceantair scrúdú don Fháinne Ghlas a bheith ann. Tá mé céasta le mic léinn ag fiosrú fá dheacrachtaí; dá mbeadh siad ag fanacht le Harry Taylor** ní fhéadfadh siad bheith níos míshuaimhní. Molaim go mór díograis na lads seo mar tá sé thar a bheith deacair, ní hamháin staidéar anseo, ach litir a scríobh de bharr an síor-racáin. Ní ag agóid atá mé nó ní fhéadfá bheith ag súil go rachadh na stócaigh thart ar nós manach, ach ós rud é nach gceadaítear peil ná aon spórt eile, ní thig liom ach bheith den bharúil gurb é an rún ag an rialtas sinne a chur as ár meabhair nó ár gcoinneáilt ó bheith páirteach i gcúrsaí polaitíochta. Cuir i gcás, agus mé ag scríobh anois tá Raidió Éireann ag cur ceol rince ar fáil, díospóireacht taobh thiar díom fá ghirseach éigin, duine ag obair ar phíosa adhmaid. Ná bígí den bharúil gur teach na ngealt atá anseo. Réitímid go maith lena chéile,

* Seán Ó Dí, *i.e.* John Bull: Sasana.
** Cigire RUC Brainse Specialta (*Feach fonóta ar leathanach 65*).

ach tuigfidh sibh, b'fhéidir, cad chuige a bhfuil muid i gcónaí ag iarraidh tuilleadh bothán taobh istigh de na clósanna gidh go bhfuil siad millteanach beag mar atá siad.

Glacaimid leis, ar an chomhairle go bhfuil dualgas trom orainn achan íobairt a dhéanamh chun cuidiú leis na fir cur i gcoinne na ndálaí seo, ach ar a bharr sin tuigimid gur seans é seo córas oideachais fhiúntaigh a chur ar fáil chomh maith. Dár ndóigh, níl an rialtas dall air seo ach oiread, mar sin de chuir siad achan seort constaice inár mbealach nuair a thoisigh muid ag iarraidh ranganna staire, matamaitice, Béarla, Rúisise - gach ábhar a d'iarr na fir orainn a chur sa tsiúl daofa. An tseachtain seo caite tháinig ionadaithe ó ghrúpa de mhúinteoirí scoile chugainn, iad lánsásta cuidiú linn an córas oideachais a thoiseacht. Deir siad linn go bhfuil 150 acu ann. Anois níl tuilleadh leithscéalta fágtha ag an rialtas; thig linn dul ar aghaidh - nó shílfeá sin - ach ar maidin nuair a phléigh mé an cheist leis an leasghobharnóir, rinne sé gearán liom nár chuala sé tada go fóill ó na státseirbhísigh in Stormont. Ní eisceacht í seo ach bunchuid de shaol an champa. Ní nach ionadh go gcailleann na fir a míthapa leis go bairdéirí go minic.

I ndeireadh na dála is dócha gurb é seo an buaireamh is mó atá ar an Chomhairle: go bhfágfaidh na fir an poll ifreannda seo slán i gcorp agus in intinn. Ní féidir a shéanadh chuile lá a dtig go n-éiríonn an teannas níos measa. In amanna is féidir é a mhothachtáil go fisiciúil chóir a bheith. Is beag áit in Éirinn nó thar lear, má tá Éireannaigh ann, nár chuala daoine trácht ar an Cheis Fhada. Is é is mó atá ar m'intinn na laethe seo (agus ar intinn go leor eile sa champa nach braighdeanaigh iad) nach rachaidh an scéal amach maidin éigin go raibh círéib anseo agus gur maraíodh méid uafásach fear. Is maith go bhfuil clú agus cáil ar an Cheis Fhada, ach go sábhála na déithe muid ó lá den chineál sin.

Latest Camp Shuffle Leads to Rural-Urban Confrontation

L AST WEEK WAS INDEED bizarre; there are times when one has the faintest of hints that the world is, in fact, constructed along Kafkaesque lines. These clues to the irrational underworld that every so often threatens to erupt are never so compelling as to force one immediately to seek the shelter of an asylum, but they are very disturbing.

Sunday was a particularly glorious day. The sun shone, birds actually twittered, in the distance the Lisburn hills wore a gentle haze: Monday, hailstones fairly lashed the camp, bitter cold winds sneaked round the huts, cutting through umpteen layers of clothing. Very disturbing, particularly as there are four peculiar civilians wandering around questioning the warders. They arrived accompanied by a plush caravan which is irritating the senior officers who must transact their duties in the rain and gales. It was the caravan which first attracted attention. Any new development requires immediate investigation; getting scéal is a vital part of the day's activities. Rumours naturally abounded. Some suggested that it was a response to a demand for more private visits by wives, others hoped that a bar was to be opened as part of the initiatives. The truth, well, is the truth.

The four gentlemen are members of the organisation and methods branch of the Home Office. The prison officers have been instructed to answer truthfully any and all questions. These I understand, really are extremely difficult: 'what are you doing now' or 'what did you do during the past five minutes'. The Prison Officers' Association, by the way, was not informed of what is a clear breach of even contractual employment. It probably is not too fanciful to suggest that the end product will be a significant contribution by Mr. Heath to the new order in Europe, a pamphlet entitled 'efficiency and inefficiency in the management of Concentration Camps'.

In the meantime, a member of the camp council had been probing about the reasons behind the latest internal camp shuffle. The wall of silence surrounding such moves was breached officially: the purpose is to ensure that each cage will have an adequate number of young men to enable inter-cage matches to be played.

The scheme from Sunday last actually provides for rural – urban confrontations as a number of countrymen have been confined exclusively to one area. Those who scorned this revelation have been dispersed in confusion for on Wednesday the first ball was kicked, we violated the virgin pitch. Again very disturbing.

Then one afternoon my siesta was cut short when I was asked to join a representative group of internees to meet some visiting social workers who had cajoled their way past the serried ranks of security to assist our very active, hard-pressed resident, Miss Kennedy*. We met actually inside the camp, four members of the Legion of Mary and ourselves, myself somewhat disbelieving as my capacity for scepticism has been enhanced of late. Our conversation was normal, I suppose, as we warmed to the task of enlightening our relatively naive guests as to the problems we face. The dreamlike quality was restored to the situation when our companions confessed that they had never heard of Harry Taylor**. I returned to the cage beginning to doubt the existence of the gentleman myself.

Everyone's world tends to be fairly circumscribed, horizons are fairly near at hand, although I do remember standing in Picadilly Circus and reading above a shop door 'The Hub of the Universe'. Devastating, or as we say here, there's a thing now. We are probably as guilty, in as much as it comes as a severe shock to learn that there are people in Europe (Switzerland) who understood Long Kesh to be a village with no unwilling residents. I learned this also last week as the censors seemed to conspire to promote my generalised unease by an increased flow of uncensored mail.

From France and the Comité pour la Liberation du

---

* The resident social worker, very popular with the prisoners. She allowed Des O'Hagan regular use of her office phone to keep in contact with the NICRA office.

** The well-known Inspector Harry Taylor of the RUC Special Branch, one of the main figures in repressing dissent against the Stormont regime, and who participated in the questioning and beating of internees.

Peuple Irlandais came a three-page report on a mass demonstration held in Place de la République on February 10th. Apparently eight thousand demonstrators condemned the Derry massacre and called for an end to both internment and the Special Powers Act. Their petition was signed by such notables as Satre, de Beauvoir, supported by numerous lawyers, writers and academics. Their slogans avoided the usual clichés, were brutally direct so that the reader was left in no doubt about their opinions: *Heath! Salaud! La peuple aura ta peau!* *, which I have laboriously discovered is a fairly decent popular sentiment. It would not have missed the gouging blue pencil had it been in Gaelic.

A letter from Rome arrived the following day, not from the Pope, thank heavens, but from the Group for Civil Rights in Ireland, who have been active in fundraising for relief committees in Belfast and Derry. They have also held an all-night vigil in front of St. Peter's, which kind of puts sitting outside Downing Street in the shade. Is there a one-upmanship in picketing locations or possibly a league table, the Pentagon, Red Square, St. Peter's, Downing Street (now threatened with relegation)? In the light of the Unionist Party's major propaganda plans, it is cheering to know that this Italian group is disseminating information, not just locally, but also throughout Europe. It is also a pity that our home movie had not been shot by Fellini as there is considerable interest in the product, the last word in the theatre of the absurd.

To complete my unhinged feeling, I had the following

---

* A common French protest chant turned against Ted Heath (Heath! Bastard! The people will have your skin!)

letter from Essex, though paradoxically it should help to retain sanity. 'My wife and I wish to convey our sense of outrage at your imprisonment without trial. I find quite a few of my countrymen object to the injustice of your present position and are trying to impress this opinion on our Government. Speaking also as an old soldier, with two years of lousy service in France and Belgium, 1916-1918, I can assure you that time will pass when you will have long since been liberated and your present loss of freedom and 'ill-treatment' will be something most Englishmen will want to forget.' On second thoughts my queasy imitations of a world near mad look pretty silly in the warm light of this man's refusal to let the past or the present to be shaped in anything other than human terms.

Historical Footnote: Those who are interested in the dynamic intervention of social structure and political values (Long Kesh) might care to analyse the following poster which appeared in one cage prior to St. Patrick's Day. I reproduce it here without comment:

All alcoholic beverages will be pooled
and distributed equally.

How the
Shamrock was
Well Drowned

T HE ROAD TO HELL is paved with good intentions, which seems to mean an awful lot of navvys are employed on that particular building site. On Saturday, March 18th, I collapsed out of bed conscious of very little except that I had made my labourer's contribution to the broad downward highway.

I suppose on reflection that it was worth it although I would not enthuse over the previous evening's Scoraiocht so keenly as a friend who doubted whether he would rather have spent St. Patrick's Day any place else. Truthfully, there was an arm-linking comradeship in our cage, we sang songs sad and gay, laughed uproariously, cheered to the echo the winners of the day's competitions. We denied as loudly as possible everything except our pleasure in each other, the enjoyment of the for-once cheerful canteen-Nissen hut. It was a sentimental evening where we became very self-conscious, as if to provide one good memory when reminiscences of Long Kesh are swapped, for our cage has had more than its share of grief.

This letter, then, is something of a roll call not of all the men in Cage 4 but of some as they appeared in the course of the evening. This is so possibly because I feel that our festivities helped to preserve our individuality and shattered the anonymity of what is a grey world. It may also be that we were whistling loudly in the dark, if that was the case then the blackness was grim.

Unconsciously I think the canteen had taken on the appearance of one of the many shebeens which sprouted in working class Belfast after August 1969. We even had a doorman meticulously handing out two chits for the bar. I wonder now did Eddie Keenan - later he whooped out 'Follow Me Up To Carlow' - actually expect to discover gatecrashers among us, his scrutiny gave me the same uneasy feeling one has squeezing among regulars through the unwelcoming near closed door of a strange club, ready to plead an explanation as to why one should not be excused entrance. At the far end of the hut our makeshift bar, carefully guarded by Freddie Scappaticci and Angelo Morelli, provoked immediate demands for a purge of the Mafia, an end of prohibition in the camp to prevent another St. Valentine's Day Massacre. We also later began to appreciate the significance of the marriage-feast of Cana, for as the night wore on, their diminutive containers continued to flow, all were satisfied.

Johnny Collins, bespectacled eyes gleaming, marshalled the performers. He joined the first group - 'straight from a successful whirlwind tour of Girdwood, the Maidstone,

Crumlin, now resident in Long Kesh, for your entertainment exclusively, the fabulous Cat Melodeons': and the feeling was what better place could they be. The Cat, Brendan McNulty, leader of the group, was catweazle with ambitions to be a jockey, harmonising with Tony McKay and Tommy Sinclair: their fans found it hard to howl down the strong vocal support for an all Ardoyne Dylan-Donovan quintet, Kill's Cubs, the Cowboy Singers led on guitar by Thunder McAuley supported by the Brothers Kane, Brian Mullan and Mickey Moan.

Sean Murphy sang *The Foggy Dew*, starting a flood of bubbling thoughts: Father Charles O'Neill, who wrote the verses, worked in St. Peter's, twin spires black over the Falls, my mother telling me how Countess Markievicz and Father Flanagan were stoned in the shadow of the same church by irate Hibernians, Connolly, who lived next door, fighting slavery on a seldom-received pound a week so that she said, 'We borrowed cups of sugar in '13.' Then Sean McKnight, whose voice conjured up Connemara, Spideal, Fiesti Conlon, shy on the tin whistle, which brought me rushing back to the Old House Bar, the Falls Fleadh, but it is 'in Grafton Street in November we tripped lightly along the way.' We were silent as he finished.

Our table, Rodgers, Sullivan, Browning, Larkin, Campbell, cheered as loudly as any, for we are all in Hut 33, which collected, it seemed, the bulk of the prizes. We even featured in the Old Crocks' forty-yard dash, which is not to deny Willie John McCorry's victory by a stomach over Olympian Gerry Adams. Special applause was reserved for the presentation by Billy O'Neill, of the

Fáinne Glás, beaming teachers and proud pupils. So proud that Gerry Campbell claimed that he would not take a £100 for the camp-made green-wrapped ring. I do not think modern economic theory is threatened on that account in any way, but there might be something for advertisers, the promoters of enthusiasm for the language revival.

We have had many firsts here to remember and it may well be that we will all celebrate at least one birthday. But Paddy Tolan, one of the many from Ballymurphy, scored a unique hat trick on St. Patrick's Day. Not only was this his birthday, but also his wedding anniversary. I seem to recall that St. George was removed from the Vatican's official list of the canonised: our own representative seems to have fallen asleep on the job if this is how he permits his namesake to be treated. All we could do was give Paddy an extra-special roar, which just possibly may have been heard in the 'Murphy.

Everyone has a song to which they can listen again and again. 'Larkin', to my mind, has a quality which demands attention, Martin Henderson interprets it as a challenge that no longer concerns only Ireland. In Madrid, they would understand when they recall 1936 or in the States if they talk about the IWW*. 'In the month of August the bossman told us': now that is a line which I will find it hard to forget, there comes later through the good news of 'The Voice of Freedom, the Voice of Justice.' If I had thought of it at the time, 'Fair play to you Martin' would

* In 1936, the people of Madrid, aided by the International Brigades, successfully defended their capital against Franco's fascist army. The International Workers of the World (Wobblies) was founded in 1905 as a more militant form of trade unionism than that previously available.

have been the right encouragement.

There were other songs, singers, the night finished at different times. It was not for propaganda purposes that I noted an ex B Special fervently declaiming 'Who dares to say forget the past,' as some of us drifted out to the huts. We wandered back and forth reluctantly.

I am reminded now of closing time. The men always last to leave. The shouted goodnights without the slamming car doors or high laughter. Our cage area is a desolate place even in the sun. When the huts were barred the patrolling soldiers must have felt a little lonelier.

A Great
Week for
Craic

THERE ARE TIMES WHEN the craic is absolutely great. Most of the debates which take place are the usual sort of chat one would come across in any half-decent bar on a Saturday night, but occasionally we get drunk on conversation. Last week was a great week for craic.

The tone was set by an internee's friend from Co. Tyrone: his wife, who seems to have as sharp a sense of humour as himself, was recounting local grass-roots Unionist attitudes which naturally included strong feelings about the party's leaders, particularly Mr. Faulkner.

He was described as 'that wee runt who has as many faces as a dying goat.' The village wiseman said bitterly: 'sure he ate his words, a hundred times.'

I suppose this is an apposite analysis, fitting more than the slippery ex-Prime Minister for it was clear that disillusionment with politics is not absolute. Big Ian is still a frontrunner in his district at least. 'He is the only man among them worth a damn.'

This, not surprisingly (if one knows Tyrone, which is almost as autonomous as Kerry) is attributed to the fact that he spent his formative years near Sixmilecross. 'The while as a wee 'un round the 'Cross cutened him up.' There should be widespread agreement, even in Westminster, on that statement.

Mr. Craig, I am afraid, can take no consolation from Tyrone opinions in his attempt to go one up on the Civil Rights Association. Vanguard is very far back in the estimation of the farmers. No wonder, as the two-day strike caused the deaths of thousands of chickens and a massive loss of milk. Mr. Craig might find, if he moved outside of his fairly narrow circle of advisers, that his disruption campaign was as fruitless as that initiated by others in a violent manner.

A second major talking point was another campaign, this time propaganda. A local paper carried a story of an illegal radio claiming a radius of twenty five miles, calling itself 'The Workers' Radio,' and organised by the Official Republican Movement.

I think the whole camp was trying to beam in on their broadcast. We were lucky. Very faintly at first could be heard the harsh Belfast voice announcing record requests from wives, girlfriends, mothers. It did not really matter that we had heard the song on a hundred different occasions, the men strained, angrily hushing any late comers to the group. 'That so and so, in Cage Five ... whist ... was that Billy from the Markets' girlfriend?' The reception could be improved, we discovered, by pressing down on top of the radio, so we perched it as high as possible on a locker, earthed by the weight of an internee.

It was local radio; many would say it was blatant illegal propaganda. One can understand and even sympathise with this point of view. The young nervous voices, stumbling, hesitant, were quietly sincere, stating their faith in ordinary people, in the hope of Roman Catholic and Protestant working-class unity; I see in the intent listening eyes, agreement. (The Gaeltacht radio should consider employing local people in similar capacity. They have a natural style which professionals seem to lack.)

Naturally, Friday was the day. A close friend was one of the first to be released. He had been offered a conditional discharge months previously, but had refused to give the undertaking which was demanded at the time – one of four men who courageously turned their backs on those open gates.

I was hauled out of bed to shout hoarse farewells across the wire, it may have been simply that I was not fully awake, but there was not much to say. He looked as dazed as I felt, whitefaced, eyes shining, his suitcase bulging with eight months of books, hopes and ideas.

The excitement was passed on by look, touch, voice, the air: men who liked to meditate late in bed crowded near the gates exchanging shouted names with other cages. Even the officers were affected by the holiday atmosphere. As the morning passed rumours hastily revised the numbers to an unlikely total of releases: the fact that we thought any figure unlikely possibly reflects the extent to which we have been institutionalised. One almost begins to accept internment. It stopped at 43, a trickle poured on the arid, bloody soil of the North.

Although we, like most others, had been waiting on this step, and are mentally adjusted, tonight the camp has the same empty quality as on the Sunday of the Derry massacre. Men went to bed early, withdrawing to their own haven. There is a stillness in the hut and emotional exhaustion; one small group remains whispering loudly, others toss, restless, cough. It will, I feel, be a long night for many. Old hands who have passed this way before know that now is the most awful time. Expectations raised bring thoughts of home, each call to the Governor's office could be that call. Nerves stretched, taut, whip back lashing others into ready anger. In some ways, though, it must be easier for us than those who wait on the outside. For women, harassed in so many different ways, each release into their neighbourhood, the joy of others, the jubilation to see someone else reclaimed, there must be agony.

The long trek back to Long Kesh, the waiting, the brief visit, the crying children, this surely must be heartbreak.

Our worries have been routinised, we know the irritants, and most times can laugh, at any rate ultimately, at the pettiness of bureaucracy. We have the company of men whose insights keep us interested, talking: in fact, not only last week, but indeed often, the craic is great.

Worldly Affairs
That Intrude Upon
Contemplative Life

R EADING THE AUTOBIOGRAPHY OF Malcolm X, one
of the many books sent to the camp by Proinsias
Mac Aonghusa*, Malcolm is quoted as once saying, 'In the
hectic pace of the world today, there is no time for
meditation or deep thought. A prisoner has time that he
can put to good use ... if he's motivated ...' The catch is in
the 'motivated', also in the extent to which one's
imprisonment is monastic. This is true for Long Kesh in
one very real sense as academics say, but mundane affairs
manage to intrude often enough to militate against
contemplation.

For example Belfast Corporation rates' department
recently requested me to attend a magistrates court to
explain why I, like thousands of other Belfast citizens, had

---

* Proinsias Mac Aonghus, Irish-language broadcaster, Irish-language activist, and
member of the Irish left.

not paid my rates. Although we arrived at a fairly amicable arrangement, based largely on the fact that I had no money, this sort of sortie by the city fathers is somewhat upsetting. This was my second visit to the outside world, the first was likewise to a court, to explain why I had 'illegal' documents in my possession, pamphlets published by Sinn Féin (Gardiner Place). The magistrate, a very discerning man, having imposed a fine of £25, allowed me ten weeks to pay. The problem is that he failed to mention how I was to manage that as the military were waiting impatiently to escort me back to Long Kesh. I am seriously thinking of drawing Mr. Whitelaw's attention to this peculiar use of the courts.

It is not only the Northern Irish courts which interest us, or at least which are drawn to our attention; two young Belfastmen are presently engaged in collecting signatures in support of a petition to secure the dropping of charges against Angela Davies. Both these lads are in contact with the London Release Committee, who sent them colourful badges calling for the freedom of all political prisoners. About 90% of the men have promised their support: there are some who refuse to sign because Angela is a committed Communist, arguing that she is part of a conspiracy to overthrow the democratically-elected government of the United States. Ronald Reagan and the other crackers can draw little comfort from this as I feel their refusal is mainly an emotional reaction to the word Communist and not based on the facts of the racialism which corrodes America.

The other petition currently circulating arises directly from the camp council. On a proposal by Gerry McKerr

(Lurgan) and seconded by myself the council has authorised the different cage representatives to collect the names of all men who are opposed to the decision of the Leinster House Government to apply for membership of the E.E.C. It is a simply-worded statement – 'We, the internees in Long Kesh, say NO to the E.E.C; we ask you to vote 'no' on our behalf in the coming referendum'. Over 500 of us have signed, not, let me emphasise, simply at the request of the council; we are too heterogeneous a group to respond almost as one man to directives. There have been furious debates as to this proposed step as we all realise the enormous implications of joining the 'Community', but in the long run all our discussions stop at the Republican charter, the 1916 Proclamation, 'We declare the right of the people of Ireland to the ownership of Ireland and to the unfettered control of Irish destinies, to be sovereign and indefeasible'. It may be naive on our part but we feel certain that membership of the E.E.C. would be contrary to this fundamental principle.

It must have been a combination of petitions, rumours and releases (these continue. I think last week eight were released) but I had a nightmare. I mean no disrespect to Dr. Martin Luther King when I write that it seemed to be similar to his words 'I have a dream'. The New Jersualem visible from the top of the hill was shrouded in mist, but I managed as I sleep-flew across to pick out some interesting details.

I could see beneath a trembling pure silk flag emblazoned Éire Nua a bar arranged to look like the map of Ireland; dark corners hidden in smoky haze apparently threatened to erupt inwards. Intuitively I suddenly understood, with the certainty of absolute knowledge, that the whole space was Dublin and that the corners were simply pulsing rhythmically to a central juke-box designed to represent the G.P.O.

The music was triumphant, a Wagnerian *Róisín Dubh*; the older customers froze between verses striking aggressive, teeth-clenched poses. A group of what appeared to be cattle dealers or successful businessmen circulated back-slapping, flushed with food, wine, joviality, snapping figures at sweating waiters. Obviously, a party was in progress.

I drifted closer. A number of men, uneasy, clutching glasses nervously, strained, fixed smiles, were being fêted: 'Jasus, but you're great lads up there in the North,' jerking his big head, but I could see nothing in that direction. 'Fair play to ye, no better men, drink up.' He stopped, looked fierce, 'It's the Republic.' Some young girls joined him tittering, frowning anxiously as he thumbed over his shoulder at the fading group he had just left.

The rest of the dream was even more confused: it seemed as if the baked interior of one building was entirely draped in flags hanging in rows linked to a maze. The impression I now have was of a vast mausoleum leading to a dimly lit courtyard; this in turn changed into a series of small backyards occasionally lit by the glow from bedroom windows. In the distance a dog was barking fiercely, the sound echoed round the yard, so that it seemed to come from an overflowing waste bin. The streets in this part of town were deserted, as, for some reason, I frantically rushed, twisting and dodging, back to the bar. (It seems that I awoke the internee in the bunk above me at this point.)

Now I recognised a few faces. Squashed in the corner, they were trapped by the press of the crowd; reluctantly, I was drawn to them. Clearly afraid of attracting attention we were pushed to and fro, further and further away. The movement was no longer accidental, the faces were threatening, bulging eyes, shouting, as we backed off. The dream changed abruptly as dreams do, yet preserved continuity. We wandered aimlessly, with many others on a cold, windswept plain. The man walking beside me was about to tell me why we were there when one of our early risers awoke me.

Normally my sleep is untroubled and my friends to whom I have told the story feel that I have composed this dream, except the man in the top bunk. He demands that I put my name down for the doctor or else move to a new bed.

Image-Builders 'Sensationalist' in their Portrayal of Joe McCann

Hollywood Character Emerges

JOSEPH MCCANN* IS DEAD. I intended to write something else at this point but what immediately comes into my mind are lines from a song of the Wobblies, 'It's there you'll find Joe Hill ... but Joe says I, you're ten years dead, I never died says he.'

Possibly the words are in the wrong order, in fact may not even be the proper words, but the sentiment is what we who knew Joe McCann feel. The press tried to create

---

* Joe McCann, a staff captain of the Belfast Command of the IRA, and education officer and public relations officer of the Liam Mellows Republican Club in south Belfast, was unarmed when he was murdered by British troops on April 15, 1972. A photo of him wielding the Starry Plough and an M1 carbine during fighting the night internment was introduced was published worldwide, and became an iconic image of the Troubles. His huge funeral attendance was addressed by Cathal Goulding.

what I feel is an obscene myth where there was a man, possibly more correct it was a section of the press which felt the need to peddle sensationalism to a public to whom violent death is no longer shocking; their crude efforts to make a flashy Damon Runyon* character of Joe were sickening. They derived from what seemed to be conscious attempts to portray the struggle of people (any people) as a Hollywood gangster film; human tragedies do not conform to Bogart-style scenarios, and it is truly sad when journalists, automatically it seems, write as if the world were but an extension of a shabby film lot.

It may be a gratuitous insult to Americans but in spite of their many wonderful contributions on film the responsibility for such shoddy shallowness is largely theirs, although indeed there must be many in the U.S.A. who are more frightened of this dimension of their power than by the awfulness of their weaponry.

They would be right, for the image builders, whatever their reasons, although wrong in their portrayal of Joe McCann, unfortunately would have created a caricature which many will accept because they have seen it so often on television and, alas, probably identified with it.

Many times here in Long Kesh we have been stunned by news, Derry's Bloody Sunday, the Abercorn Restaurant, McGurk's bar; on this occasion I noticed that the men kept hoping, even when the story was no longer unconfirmed rumour, that somehow or other, it was just not true. Yet once accepted the mood changed abruptly. I am told that cloistered religious celebrate a death, I think

* Damon Runyon was an American author who specialised in writing about larger-than-life characters and gangsters in New York.

it is true to say in the same way that we may have felt something approaching gaiety, as if we understood that Joe's death was a releasing of the pent-up, crushed, battered spirit of the people.

It may have been the manner of his death. A brief wild chase, the dash for the security of the Market slums, the billowing overcoat, the quick orders to halt, the crackling of gunfire, the twist and fall, the closing crescendo to kill, this was ritual execution acted out by many throughout the history of the Irish people.

It is caught on the wind, it reaches into our memories stirring dread and wonders, half-recollected stories heard from brooding proud men at street corners on dark winter evenings or in the glow of turf fires throwing sudden giants on the wall, daubing the mind. Somehow there is satisfaction, one can picture knowing old men, anger thin in their blood, nodding with little tender secret smiles. How else could it be, how else would it be, for those who were and are our heroes?

From Cúchalain to Mellows, in mythology and reality, those whom we acknowledge to be great have faced overwhelming odds, never despairingly, but because it could not be any other way. But they have always reassured us by being human, we have no Mount Olympus even Slemish is only a hump on the ground, they have been fiercely linked to the people and although they have died in the canon's mouth, we remember them not as soldiers but as men.

We cherish their imperfections, the proofs of their humanity because as people we have suffered much at the Nitzschean figures from Cromwell to Churchill. If we are to be criticised, it is because we have been too generous with the lives of those who wish only to provide for the people, Connolly bleeding in a chair for the exploited working class, Mellows shot for giving the land to the peasants, now Joe McCann for believing that only the people should have power, to be sure it is usually the English who provide the martyrdom but we are too eager to welcome it.

Many have died in this past twelve months, there have been ugly, bloody, murderous deeds perpetrated through sectarian hatred; distrust, fear, violence divide the working class. I like to think that Joe's death, as his life, being in the only tradition which offers hope to the people will in some way be a cleansing influence. The men here who are in the same tradition know the explosive combination of unemployment, poor housing, inferior education, many have actually fought against sectarianism through Republican Clubs in company with Joe, but it came as a surprise even to learn that Gusty Spence in Crumlin Road Prison this past seven years, had written to Mrs McCann offering his sympathy and telling how he had not forgotten a kindness done to him by Joe. We do not know what this was but it surely must offer hope for that section of the people who have suffered most when a Shankill Road Loyalist identifies with a dead Republican leader from Turf Lodge.

In Divis Flats, the Markets, Ballymurphy, some day also in Sandy Row, Dee Street, the Shankill where over-worked women and workless men, powerless, manipulated, now begin to stir listlessly, there will be recognition that Joe McCann stood out against mindless sectarian hatred, that his life was lived building not destroying but, in working for and with the people, he was making them aware of what the future could hold if they only could see to shape it.

Now it seems Utopian to talk of the day when the mass of the people have put aside contrived differences, rejected demonic leadership and begun to build a truly human society in which men will be valued by what they can give and receive according to their needs. That vision has been with us a long time, it did not perish with Tone, Lalor, or Connolly, it did not die in Joy Street with Joe McCann, if anything it has become brighter, warmer, nearer and in its coming we can hear a growing, swelling, rising song of the people: ... *I never died said he.*

Widgery*:
Shock to Believers
in Fair Play

T HERE ARE TIMES WHEN I am almost totally inclined
to the view that the English do not really believe in
justice, honour, decency, the principles of democracy, fair
play and the other virtues which they know too well are
unfortunately absent in most, if not all, foreigners.
Widgery is an example which must sadly confuse everyone
who retains any affection for British standards of justice.
In fact it is nearly impossible to accept that a
distinguished, senior judge wrote the report and arrived at
the conclusions he did in the light of the evidence
presented.

Personally, I was educated to respect the empirical
tradition. I was convinced that in general it permeated all
the British social and political institutions: this led me to

---

* The Widgery Report (April 1972) whitewashed the events of Bloody Sunday,
and falsely claimed that those murdered had been using weapons.

the undignified corollary that the Irish were emotional, partisan, subjective, well-nigh incapable of arriving at a reasonable judgment. I may have been singularly naive here, but there are many in exalted political positions who are uncomfortably close to this position.

The shock of Widgery, I think, should have brought home to us not only the foolishness trusting in national stereotypes but also the need to review Anglo-Irish relationships from an entirely different perspective. Last week some of us began this difficult exercise starting with the present 'spontaneous' demands for peace, honestly trying to relate them to the Heath initiative.

One member of our group stated that he was reminded at this time of a comment by his mother during a radio broadcast of the Rinty Monaghan-Jackie Patterson world title fight. The bout was interrupted by the announcer apologising for a short break in transmission due to technical problems. Reporting from the King's Hall, Belfast would be resumed as soon as possible.

The good woman not being too well informed of the nature of such broadcasts proclaimed warmly that she was sure that the two fellas would be glad of the break, God help them. This is just about how the present situation seems to us now.

I doubt very much if there is one man in Long Kesh who does not genuinely desire peace. The cynical may interject that this is a belated conversion, a baptism to be welcomed as long as the converts are not allowed to preach their gospel. One cannot possibly convince anyone holding such a view, as in all probability they believe that the violence done to internees was justified: if internment camps are necessary to prevent desirable social change then by all means have them. Anyhow our commitment to peace is not simplistic. I have been surprised by the heightened political awareness shown not by the members of our discussion group but by all the men to whom I have access. Naturally enough we are anxious that this camp should be available as soon as possible (immediately) to lovers in parked cars, that the tinkers should be seen scavenging eagerly among the deserted Nissen huts.

At the same time no-one is happy that his freedom should be threatened continually by the Special Powers Acts. Alarming stories of heavily armed soldiers paying a friendly visit to released internees to ensure that they keep their noses clean are commonplace. Such courtesies one can understand taking place in the East End of London, where it is simply a matter of a benign 'evening-all' bobby keeping a humane eye on a returned tearaway.

Undoubtedly the fact that the Six County Executive of Republican Clubs recently held a public convention in Belfast attended by Tomás Mac Giolla, president of Sinn Féin without interference from the security forces would seem to indicate that our scepticism as to the future may be groundless. What would reassure more than the phasing out of internment would be the introduction of a bill of rights guaranteeing unimpeded access to the political space.

Last week, talking to delegates from the World Peace Council, who visited the camp about the present repressive legislation, internment and the denial of the rule of law, I found myself presenting the democratic case, describing the antipolitical character of our society as if I did not expect to be believed. One becomes almost apologetic as the description of events and practices seems to belong more to the early days of the Third Reich than to part of the present United Kingdom. Mr. Krishna Menon intervened to point out, quietly, sincerely, that once courts were corrupted by the executive then it was only a matter of time until all human freedoms were denied. Democracy cannot be administered like medicine, one apparently either kills the patient or cures him.

Our present state of suspended animation, he was surprised to learn, did not include a total ban on what is usually described as subversive literature. When I returned to Cage 2 I thought it might be of interest to examine the books we have in the hut. The list makes ironic reading and is an index of the extent to which the law has become a matter of taste in Northern Ireland, for possession of many of the books now in Long Kesh is an offence under the Special Powers Act. On the other hand, it is probably more fruitful to see this as a chink in the grey clouds of political censorship which for so long have hung over the North.

Here it must be admitted we could learn from the English not only in Belfast but also in Dublin.

Three into one does go after all. Sunday last saw the transfer of the seventy-eight Magilligan men, to Long Kesh. Cage 10 houses the new arrivals. Cage 9 the men transferred from the Maidstone a few weeks ago. This seems to complete phase three of the Long Kesh expansion programme. As far as I can gather, it means in fact that we will have a holy trinity of camps under one supreme authority, Mr. Truesdale. There are rumours though that numbers 11 and 12 are in the course of construction but I doubt if it will be possible to confirm this as the sites are so far removed from this end of the complex that I understand small electric buggies will be used to ferry meals to the internees expected there.

Release by
Russian Roulette
or R.R.C.?

O N A WET WINDY day there are drearier places in Ireland than the black flooded runways of Long Kesh, but from where I sit in the new small 'quiet-hut' the view is decidedly depressing. Looking left between two grey Nissen huts my eyes picked up discarded orange skins, pieces of sodden wrapping paper, then the boundary fences festooned with coiled barbed wire (we have thought of training roses to grow along these thorns. Sorry) and come to rest on the square red iron gate supports which lead into other complexes.

This physical slice of the site is today cupped by a bleak dark northern sky. It is also Monday, the beginning of another week in which we will commiserate nine months of captivity, a fair oul time as the man said. Overall it is the sort of day when it is ruefully aware of what we half affectionately refer to as the Big D, described by the Red

Cross as a falling in morale, a general air of depression.

Paradoxically this mood, I think, has increased of late, one hears more complaints of headaches, some voices seem shriller, more quickly raised in annoyance, while others withdraw into protective silence. This is a response, not just to the releases of the past few weeks but equally to the manner of the releases. Tuesday, Wednesday, Thursday have displaced visits from home as tension high points of the week, for it is on these days shortly after two o'clock when the entire camp is agitated by the appearance of a deputy governor, accompanied by the senior prison officers responsible for each cage. Cages 2, 3, 4, 5 are a half circle with the administration block in the centre so that the men living in this area are aware almost immediately if anyone is to go free.

The procedure has become finalised. The deputy governor, holding a thin sheet of startlingly white paper, enters the cage: he remains poised, indifferent at the gate as the senior prison officer directs a warder to fetch an internee. At the door of each hut a small crowd has gathered, watching self-consciously. Each man feels his stomach lurch sickeningly as the guard approaches; never did any actor play his role so dramatically: the called name unlocks a sad hub-bub of applauding shouts. It may be two or even three who pack away their bedding on a wooden truck surrounded by friends, their joy edged with pain.

Faced with this sadistic system of release by Russian roulette, we have responded by endeavouring to overcome the massive alienation it engenders by pretending either to be in control or at least able to explain the basis on which releases occur. In our cage, from which quite a number of men have been freed, we have fabricated a few reasonable myths and an all-powerful body which decides who is to go next. Let me state categorically now that if any of our friends on the outside have heard rumours that this group is in any way connected with or influenced by the Southern establishment they can accept my assurance that these are absolutely untrue. Naturally enough, I cannot speak for whatever other agencies exist within the camp.

One bed in one hut was coveted for a time, as successive occupants were called to better things: at the moment it lies fallow as current long odds suggest that its fruitfulness is exhausted, having delivered so many winners. We have also turned to other worldly affairs in our search of explanations: for a time participation in the rosary was considered to be a gilt-edged security but the recent success of men who bore Our Lady of Fatima, in statue form, round the cages has caused considerable anxiety as this was a once-off procession. There is also thriving speculation with regard to the men who were fortunate to shake the hand of the Cardinal, in the flesh, on his recent pastoral visit to the camp. Odds here are very short indeed, though usually well-informed sources discount any possible connection between his call here and his later meeting with Mr. Whitelaw.

Wully Whitewash*, as they have endearingly baptised him on the Shankill Road, might be interested in a little bit of grassroots Unionist gossip from Co. Tyrone which came my way last week on the whole subject of internment. (My informant from that region has now

* William Whitelaw, Secretary of State for Northern Ireland.

rejoined his family, more power to him). 'Faulkner was the greatest devil that we ever had, he ruined the country by bringing in internment. We are free of him now and we can do as we like, we were tied to people like him but we are not tied now.' It is not that I can see droves of loyalist farmers flocking into the Civil Rights Association, heralding a new age of emancipation and enlightenment, but when one compares the basic good sense of that statement with the urbane idiocy of Enoch Powell's recent aside that the cause of violence is the belief that it will succeed, I, like many more, would rather look west of the Bann for guidance than to Oxbridge chauvinists within the Tory Party, not that we are likely to influence them, or they us.

Our all-powerful body which I mentioned earlier makes the decisions as to whom is to be released and when. Known as the Revolutionary Release Committee it has a revolutionary chairman and secretary, issues daily bulletins and spends a considerable amount of its time warding off the counter-revolutionary alliance, which is headed by a disgruntled trade unionist who claims that the original committee was never elected. Acceptance, however, is not based in this case on democratic origins but on successful forecasting. So far the R.R.C. has not only maintained its position but staggered the opposition by having the revolutionary secretary released.

It is still raining, rumours abound, one third of the camp is expected to close before the end of the month but this week the major talking point has been the E.E.C. and the destruction of the Belfast Co-operative Stores. As yet I have met no-one who has expressed approval of such an act, although I dare say there are some who can be found to defend it, just as there are those who can be found to defend internment.

A day in the life of Long Kesh . . .

Monstrous Rhythm
Interrupted
Only by Sleep

I HAD A STIMULATING LETTER last week from an old lady in Donegal who, apparently sensing that I was somewhat depressed, sat down and wrote 17 exuberant pages of scandal, gossip and yarns about people whom I do not even know. It was indeed a great tonic. She asked me to write in detail about a day in Long Kesh, what we do, as she said, morning, noon and night.

As the days have become routinised or, as old prison hands have it, 'the penny has dropped, you're doing time now,' it is very hard to perceive change, to note differences. We seem to be living to a monotonous rhythm interrupted, if one can call it that, only by sleep. Internees are like duppies, the living dead of West Indian mythology; in fact in my hut there are one or two who are almost a near living confirmation of the fable. Names I dare not mention for security reasons. My security.

At any rate I have had to shake myself and as I am not accustomed to keeping a diary I hope that the following notes are a reasonable account, not too crude for devotees of Samuel Pepys.

2.30 am: My feet are beginning to feel cold sitting here at the top of the hut with three others. Hut rules demand that lights are extinguished by one o'clock: anyone wanting to read or talk sotto voce must gather under one light. Occasionally someone will roar for quiet, but tonight the only sounds are from the sleepers. Last light out, bed, time to think, though not really, too disjointed, must be the infamous stream of consciousness, helicopter taking off, wake the bloody dead, still did have one trip swooping up from Crumlin across the Falls' redevelopment gaps, redevelopment nothing, must be ready to build more tower blocks now, wonder how the housing action is going, no Falls left by the time we get out, cigarettes there, lighter ...

7.30 am: I always snap awake but never at this time, the hut door has jammed so the officers are pushing, twisting at the lock. A very bright morning. Two warders counting up one side, down the other as I watch from one eye. Definitely should get up, a surge of childhood guilt, a sin to lie in bed on a fine day like this. Doze off again.

10.45 am: The voice of authority, democratically elected, now rouses the men still in bed; most of us. There are a few early birds, usually countrymen long accustomed to regular hours, but we generally like to greet the day slowly, warily. A cup of tea is a great help so little syndicates have sprung up sharing food parcels, taking turns to make the tea. This morning I also manage to get The Irish Times. Even though we know that there is the rest of the day to peruse the papers every day there is a demand to be among the first to read the news. Scarcity certainly creates competitiveness; combined with the present circumstances it has turned many men here into avid students of the press.

11 .00 am: Strip bed, fold blankets and sheets, which is necessary for hygienic reasons in our opinion; wash, study face, comb beard, ignoring sarcasm from the younger crew. Back in the hut I make the tea this time, more sarcasm, there has been a request (an insult to my integrity) for a list to be signed by each member of the syndicate to ensure that they all take their turn: the search for equality continues unabated. Conversation now revolves around the treatment of various news stories in different papers. At times one could almost believe the old story of the headline which supposedly featured in Belfast years ago, 'Catholic dog wins greyhound derby'.

12 .00 (or thereabouts): Dinner arrives. We study the menu carefully, reject steak, curry, pork chops, and settle for stew with mashed potatoes. The chef acknowledges our satisfaction with a gracious symbolic gesture from the security of the cookhouse door. A tedious part of the day, we read or talk until news time.

1 .30 pm: Raidio Éireann is genuinely admired for its extensive coverage of Six County affairs. (Is it not about time, by the way, that Telefís Éireann was equally

accessible to Northern viewers?) I doubt if a day has passed when the entire camp has not tuned into this news service: It may be prejudiced but I am of the opinion that it is as close to being objective in its reporting as is humanly possible.

2.00 pm (or slightly later): I think that I have said enough previously about this time, it is much too painful to dwell on it, rather like being let down on a date, so most men with romantic souls will know what it is like.

This afternoon there is a talk, followed by a discussion on religious sectarianism; this is a continuation of a debate begun some weeks ago. Now in the light of exploding sectarian blackness what was formerly a somewhat academic subject for some is a matter for urgent analysis. All we can do here is analyse. Today accusations are flung back and forth; charges of hypocrisy on many lips; overall I have the impression of just not knowing where to begin. It may be that the whole topic of religion in Ireland is so enclosed in myth, superstition and authoritarianism, or that it lends itself so readily to sloganising, that we find it difficult to talk rationally about sectarianism. In the prevailing climate of opinion in the North – we are part of it – to reject Roman Catholic or Protestant bigotry is simply to invite the charge of being Communist, but I have a vague memory of a bishop in South Africa saying that the only possible position for a Christian in his country was to identify with the Communists. God help him if he had lived in Ireland, Senator McCarthy was only a boy scout compared with some of our responsible citizens.

4.30 pm: There are a few who gather expectantly around the television waiting on the daily appearance of their number one pin-up Miss Helen of UTV's 'Romper Room'. It would be too much to say that she has displaced Róisín Dubh in the eyes of her admirers, but she certainly would draw a queue to the stage door if people still do that sort of thing.

Our television committee is constantly confronted with competing claims which in the last resort can never really be satisfactorily resolved but it is clear that there are priorities: current political programmes have the largest audiences, closely followed by all forms of sport, while viewing distasteful to Malcolm Muggeridge* has an excellent following. As we argue the merits of different channels, interruptions by the disgruntled are greeted with shouts of 'Who rattled your cage'? Linguists should be interested in the fact that we have generated our own rhetorical questions, for example, 'What are you wirelessing about?', directed at anyone complaining unnecessarily. This has a crushing effect, particularly when it is enunciated in a broad Belfast accent. No-one has yet produced a suitable reply.

4.45 pm: Following the Six County news bulletin, a lull in the conversation is broken by the one sentence litany, 'Big Murphy was arrested today': response, 'Aye, but he was arrested at the gate.' As Big Murphy has never been in Long Kesh the ironic historic awareness of the comment is worthy of specific origin:

---

* Malcolm Muggeridge was an author and media personality who regularly denounced what he saw as the decline in society's morals, especially sexual morals.

alas, we have failed to chart Murphy's career here precisely; we know of him as owning a chair in which one dare not sit but now that he has gone no one knows from where he came, how long he was here or in which prison his spirit now frets.

To be continued . . .

. . . second half of a day
in the life of Long Kesh

Mice Threaten
to Take Over
from Internees

6.00 PM: MARSHALL MCLUHAN* WAS half right in picturing the world as a global vilage. The tragedy of Vietnam flickers nightly, disasters such as the Battersea fun fair momentarily evoke sympathy yet it is true that we wait for the Northern Ireland news impatient with the visual horrors of An Loc** or the complexities of the British Rail dispute. Apart from the natural parochial and

---

* Marshal McLuhan was a professor of English literature who helped pioneer the academic study of popular culture and the new field of media studies. He published / coined the phrase 'the global village'.

** Five children were killed in an accident on a rollercoaster in Battersea fun fair on May 30, 1972. An Loc was a major battle of the Vietnam War that lasted from April to July 1972.

political interest in our own affairs, I think that we assess all news items as impinging adversely or otherwise on our own position. Such selfishness is understandable particularly as we study the stamping rows of the Ulster Defence Association and their efficient patrolling of weekend barricaded East Belfast.

Some of us drift away to discuss the news, others debate the merits of the evening's programmes. Undoubtedly television keeps us informed, educates us and entertains, but we seem to be dominated by its presence. It beams down from a shelf above one door: we gather underneath it like some preliterate tribe fascinated by the magical gyrations of the witch doctor. It is not really as bad as that but gradually we begin to empathise with the Luddites.

7.00 pm: Tonight our Republican Club meeting is lively. Now all discussions seem eventually to turn to sectarianism, civil war, and the growing bitterness of which we occasionally learn on visits. Encapsulated as we have been for many months in Long Kesh our analysis of the present situation is highly academic, although we all have detailed stories of Unionist 'moderates' who have become extremists during the past ten months. At times, though, we cannot help but wonder if there are now so many ex-moderates how it was that Unionism was for so long a thriving, unhealthy, sectarian, near-Fascist force in Northern Ireland. It may be that we are naive in musing thus and that the bombing has been so gross as to have rent the fabric of our community beyond patching, but as human beings we cannot accept such pessimistic futurology. Our meeting, at any rate, concluded hopefully as someone pointed out that it was still possible for ex-

extremist Unionists to join with democrats in rejecting the unjust repressive system to which we are heirs.

9.00 pm: No point in watching the news after we hear the headlines, a repeat of six o'clock. A walk round the cages is pleasant now as the evenings are brighter, warmer. The red roof of a barn on a nearby hill momentarily glows dully as car headlights move swiftly down the encircling M1. Tonight a soldier lonely in the watchtower immediately above and behind Cage 2 shouts something incomprehensible but vaguely mocking. We stop, also welcoming the opportunity to engage in an exchange of insults, glad of the 'diversion'. It took us some time to realise that this sort of heckling which the occasional guard will initiate was really stemming from a desire to establish human contact. Concerned obviously with not losing face in case the response from an internee would be too brutal the solider is forced to open a conversation across the wire in the only way possible for him, a shouted insult. We have learned in the main from these conversations something of the dimensions of British Army internal propaganda and the uneasy distaste which higher ranks have for these transient associations.

In the course of one discussion with a young soldier he told us that he had been lectured as to how we were all mad gunmen intent on murdering Protestants. I doubt if he really believed this as he was quick to relate the points we made about the nature of repression in Northern Ireland to the Heath anti-trade union policy in Britain. Our growing mutual interest was interrupted by the telephone in his box, a brief exchange and he shouted down that he had been warned to tell us to sod off. It must indeed be a poor sort of army that is afraid of its men being indoctrinated by the prisoners over whom they watch.

9.45 pm: We have a miniature billiard table donated by a sympathiser which circulated between the three huts, this week it is our turn. A knockout competition left me completely shattered. Having started favourite in the betting, evidence of my youthful wild oats, I was knocked out in the first round. One does not mind being beaten but the score was such as to leave me totally incapable of ever boasting in the future of my early prowess with a billiard cue.

12.15 am: Set the trap. We are plagued, as I mentioned once, with mice, but from wild accounts of size from those who wake in the night disturbed with revels, we are going to need this jumbo-size mark II Long Kesh guillotine-type mouse disposer. Like a part of Belfast which is renowned as the only area in which the tinkers organised a petition to have the residents removed, there are those among us who firmly believe that the mice are organising in secret and increasingly in public to force through demands to have the internees restricted to a section of the hut. The rest of the area is already almost no-go, so it would only be a matter of recognising their creeping possession of the territory. Anyway a unique trap has been ingeniously constructed. It consists of the wooden dome cover taken from a sewing machine, one end has been removed and replaced with a transparent shutter. A hole pierced through the centre is wedged with a match which itself is held in place by a length of cord running along the roof of the dome then through another hole into the trap. A hunk of cheese acts as a weight and a bait. The trap really is an architectural masterpiece. The inventor, James Lawlor, of Turf Lodge, has decided not to apply for patents, an altruistic gesture which I hope the authorities will recognise as a part of the initiatives in this post-Faulkner era. Success in the first twenty-four hours, we feel, has been good, although this judgment may be biased, for we can only guess at the total mouse population. So far, two have been detained. One managed to escape, gross negligence, which is being thoroughly investigated by the SMIB5 (Special Mouse Investigation Branch).

1.00 am: No enthusiasm tonight for late polemics, reading or the ongoing post mortem since Mr. Whitelaw arrived some ten weeks ago. Clearly, the men were adversely affected by the sudden cessation of release last week.

Time for a final cup of tea and what else can one write, but so to bed.

Historical Footnote: The recent arrival of fifty or so unfortunate short-term prisoners into one of the cages must have presented a major headache for whoever is legally responsible for their general well-being in the Ministry of Home Affairs. Apart from visits, employment, welfare, there was also the problem that Long Kesh is, after all, an internment camp. One could hardly have prisoners transferred here to serve sentences. The solution is on a notice board outside Cage 6, which, I am told, reads: H.M. *Prison, The Maze.* I suppose it is as good a name as any in the circumstances, but someone soon is certain to draw comparisons with another notorious racecourse, which could possibly prove embarrassing at Strasbourg.

Probing the
Sources of
Communal Hatred

T HAT THIS IS THE weekend of the annual Wolfe Tone
commemoration and also, I believe, the twentyfirst
letter from Long Kesh (nineteen in the Second Official
Language) makes me feel that I should try to contribute
something memorable. Unfortunately the traditional
presentation of the key of the house has been deferred
indefinitely so the many who would have joined
enthusiastically in post-Bodenstown conviviality are
unhappily contemplating another dry weekend.

Still we can reminisce about other Bodenstowns,
conjuring up the parched throng in Sallins struggling for
paper cups and black bottles. Children darting between
parked cars, buses hooting, bands piping, flat Northern
voices, quick Cork accents, crowds trudging over the
railway bridge, small groups fervently exchanging views,
the little village for a few hours, indeed, becomes the heart

of Ireland.

In a country justly renowned throughout the world for its devotion to religion it must be something of a shock for the student of Irish affairs to learn that our secular processions outweigh religious pilgrimages in our national consciousness. Bodenstown* or the Field at Finaghy have a greater hold on our lives than Saul or Knock, and at this time it is absolutely clear that Tone's programmatic call for the unity of Protestant, Catholic and Dissenter under the common name of Irishman still remains the only hope for the future. It is equally a harsh reminder to Christians of how tragically they have failed in a country in which they have wielded so much power. I suppose it is a case of the corruption of their institutions rather than their ethics.

If my visitors are correct there was an enormous sense of relief in Belfast when the para-military Ulster Defence Association declared their intention not to erect their barricades at the weekend, to withdraw, at least temporarily, from the brink. For many it must seem as if a turning point has been reached, that the mass of the people have decided not to be dragged any further towards a sectarian massacre. The U.D.A. move, following, as it does, on the Six County Executive of the Republican Clubs' initiative, has started a ferment of discussion within the camp, although unfortunately we tend to revert to the tragedy of August 1969, a corrosive episode in Northern history.

---

* Bodenstown is the site of Wolfe Tone's grave, while the Field is where Orangemen march on July 12, where the speeches etc for the day are made and listened to.

All the memories, though, are not bitter. Apparently at one local barricade in September 1969, as a police wave length was being monitored, a patrol radioed that an ugly crowd had gathered and seemed to be heading in the direction of the nearby Roman Catholic ghetto. One of a very diligent band of vigilantes dashed down the narrow street warning excitedly that a crowd of ugly Protestants was about to attack. Had the mob proceeded they would have found the defenders overcome by laughter rather than fear.

We have been comparing notes, probing our childhood for the sources of the now overt communal fear and hatred. I hope that I will be believed when I write that during twenty years or so living on the Falls Road I was never aware of hate of Protestants. The heart of the Lower Falls, that sprawl of sweat boxes erected to satisfy the needs of nineteenth century capitalism, now being ripped out to satisfy the needs of an urban motorway contained three churches, two Presbyterian and one Roman Catholic. Looking from the Shankill Road across towards the Lagan, St. Peter's Pro-Cathedral dominated the district: at the close of a sunny day the shadow from the spires could have fallen on either of the others, they sat so close together.

On a Sunday, all proceeded peacefully to their house of worship. I remembered one of the sextons who had a standing joke with my father about giving the Sunday service on the basis of fifty percent of the collection. St. Peter's still stands. Albert Street Presbyterian Church, I understand, closed and Bertha Place has gone with the surrounding slum houses. The flour mill which overshadowed the latter has disappeared, along with the impatient Clydesdale cart-horses striking sparks fretfully off the round road stones, kidney pavers or Belfast confetti of the sectarian troubles of the 1920s. The memory of those days was recalled when someone was behind with some household task which could draw the wry comment, 'they're in on us and we haven't got a stone gathered.' But seldom did I hear any talk of Protestant – Catholic conflict.

In the mill's place is a tower block of flats and a motorway planned to act as a moving boundary between the people of the Shankill and the Falls: urban planning is seemingly based on the perpetuation of sectarian conflict.

Undoubtedly, one could romanticise one's childhood, but what is certain one did not meet or play with Protestants, in spite of the fact they lived fifty yards away. Separate educational facilities ensured separate development and while it is impossible to measure the contribution that this may have made to the present situation, it must surely demonstrate the need for a revision of local theology.

August '69 was traumatic, but the wounds were healing, or rather being healed on the shop floor and the building sites, where ecumenism is a real struggle and not a topic to be enjoyed in polite conversation with tea and biscuits. One Republican internee, an ex-shop steward, pointed out as we discussed our formative years that some time before his arrest he was accepted unreservedly by the workers as mediator and spokesman, so that occasional sectarian disturbance was resolved without too much disruption. Prior to his arrest his position had been almost totally undermined by the bombing campaign, his politics, to which his loyalist workmates has been relatively indifferent, were becoming increasingly unacceptable. It is interesting that he believes the lost ground can be regained, when it is again possible for him to work as a Republican trade unionist.

Another participant in our discussion was particularly angry, not, as is our wont, about the past, but for the future. In the very large working-class Catholic estate of Andersonstown he has calculated that sixty men have lost their jobs as a direct result of explosions. When one considers the families of these men, their friends, their acquaintances and the thousands of other workers who have suffered also, the problem for Republicans intent on propagating their political philosophy seems to him well-night insurmountable. His conclusion: they have made Republicanism a dirty word.

All of this is not to say that we are less aware of the role of Orangeism and the Unionist Party as the primary womb of sectarianism. Mr. Faulkner, who extended repression in such a tragic fashion, can claim to be one of the midwives of communal hatred. His present concern for the welfare of the North sounds uniquely hollow as he snaps petulantly at Mr. Whitelaw's heels, for there are many who remember him heroically striding down the Longstone Road* some thirteen years ago, his manner no

* Brian Faulkner was one of a number of MPs who had backed the Orange order in a dispute with the residents of the Longstone Road in County Down. The Orange Order had been banned from walking there, but when the ban was lifted in 1955 craters were blown in the road to try to prevent the march, but it failed. Faulkner triumphantly joined the march on July 12. This helped seal his reputation as a hardline unionist.

less arrogant, his purpose no less criminal, than that of the most backwoods bigot. There is, I believe, good reason to hope that the bulk of loyalist workers finally have appreciated the extent to which their traditional leaders were willing to exploit their emotions in the interest of their political and economic power. The conflicts which rage beneath the surface of traditional Unionist unity promise that future defections will not be in twos to the Alliance Party but in greater numbers in more radical directions. Our analysis concluded with some thoughts for Mr. Whitelaw, and although he is in the political tradition of Burke it may be that he is astute enough to harken to the lessons of the French Revolution as understood by Tone. His sojourn in Ireland will be brief, either by virtue of an election in England or because he has contributed to the emergence of democracy: on the other hand, should he fail to confront and reject the twin evils of sectarianism and repression it is unlikely that he will be remembered other than as an Englishmen who spent some time in Ireland.

Memories
Are Made
of This . . .

T HERE OBVIOUSLY HAD TO be a last letter from Long
Kesh although I hurry to add that, along with 370
others, I am still enjoying bed and board as a guest of the
incredible Mr. Whitelaw. If it is still the practice of the
Tory Party to take soundings to discover the grassroots'
views on potential leaders, and if the new leader is still
thought of as emerging in response to the pressing needs
of the party, then Mr. Heath must be wriggling uneasily in
his chair as he applauds his Northern Ireland manager.

At the very least Mr. Whitelaw's performance must be
provoking discussion in the elegant club rooms, distraught
with fears of a sinking pound, militant workers and
depressed election agents: how about 'Whitelaw restores
peace to a troubled Whitehall?'

Naively I had hoped that I could have the story of

taking a wry, farewell look at the rows of empty Nissen huts, the corrugated iron gates slamming shut, then hurrying to a waiting car and the final ride to freedom. It would have made a beautiful ending. We are still here and I should be grateful for the opportunity of preparing, in a very real sense, a final letter. It is not that there is any hard evidence to suggest that release will be any day now but, as the times that are in it are full of endings and beginnings; I feel constrained to contribute in the same spirit. Hence the 'Last Letter from Long Kesh.'

It is too soon to start counting the gains and losses sustained, to try to balance accounts. At the same time it would be agreed by most that internment, the camp, has been the bitter heart of this past 11 months' mad fury. Long Kesh has been cursed, praised, questioned, analysed, visited, photographed (internally and externally) and finally renamed (disguised). Many who were here will look back, remembering nostalgically the comradeship, the laughs, the fears, others unfortunately but understandably will be bitter, nurturing hate, dwelling over-long on the vicious wrong done to them.

Bitterness, hate in itself need not be destructive and there are men who could be described as leaving here full of bitterness, but who in fact have found the will to hate the evils done to people and are bitter only in their rejection of the now publically-admitted sectarian brinkmanship of former republicans and their Orange counterparts. They are a promise of a better future.

At the moment, however, we are more preoccupied with memories, already recounting half-forgotten events, the humorous and the tragic. I suppose the following story is not really funny but it can still raise a laugh at each telling. One old Belfast lady, childishly innocent of the nature of internment, was paying her first visit to the camp. The warder escorted her to the tiny box where her son was already seated at the table. She gazed at him astonished, then slowly queried: 'My God, son dear, do you just sit there all day like this?'

Even Holywood has produced its crop of stories, like the young man confronted by a Special Branch officer promising all sorts of lurid ill-treatment if he did not receive the sort of answers he required. Proceeding then more calmly he demanded to know how many were in the local defence unit. The answer is still reverberating round Long Kesh: 'What's it got to do with you? You just mind your own business.' In the circumstances, to my mind, it rates as high as any scintillating witticism from Oscar Wilde.

Subsequently, during the interrogation the detainee was frog-marched to another room to confront a close relative, the detective's objective being to elicit what alleged position the relative held in the defence group. Angrily: 'Do you know who that is?' 'Aye that's our Tommy.' 'And what's he?' Pause – indignantly: 'He's a Catholic.'

But there are those who still bear the scars of Girdwood, Ballykinlar, Holywood and the secret cells in which the science of psychology was so abused in a vicious effort to dehumanise. This cannot be forgotten and as it reminds us that absolute power corrupts absolutely, it also should surely be a guarantee that special powers have no future in Ireland. Government functions, if not better, certainly less dangerously when their every action is subject to the fullest publicity.

It is hard actually to grasp that, while we have been entombed for nearly 11 months, over 300 people died violently and that many thousands were injured grievously, but we are in sufficient contact with reality to know that recent overtures to the Unionist working class from leading Provisional spokesmen who are abysmal in their political ignorance and apparently blind to their own history have absolutely no chance of being accepted. At the same time protestations from Unionist leaders of their concern for the establishment of a democratic society ring equally hollow as they continue to rant in terms of a Protestant majority and a Roman Catholic minority. If there is to be a new Ireland it can only be by way of a frontal assault on all sectarian forces combined with an end to repression.

Alternatively, we could all adopt the principle as did one internee, if you cannot beat them, join them. Certainly we were sceptical about his sanity but this is what he did. Having seen the many advertisements for the prison service he decided to apply, the application forms were delivered to his home address and were later followed by an invitation to an interview. In the meantime he was released and as far as we can learn has been accepted as a trainee prison officer. For a time there was great speculation that he would return ultimately to Long Kesh so that we gave a new twist to the old joke, 'Nut returns as screw and internees bolt for cover.'

The Camp Riot: The sad young soldier with the guard dog after the riot in October, 1971, who sneaked up to the cages to whisper that, 'One of your blokes have been murdered'. It was not true but I shall always remember his anxiety and sorrow with gratitude.

Christmas: The little girl singer standing shyly, lost, in the bitter cold dusk waiting on the cage gates being opened.

Bloody Sunday: The stillness, the shock, the sickness.

St. Patrick's Day: An angry exchange about Irish-Americans bleeding publicly for the old sod but blind to the white racist character of their adopted country.

Easter: The sharp bright notes of the Last Post.

Above All: The people at home, in England, and throughout the world, who wrote and continue to write.

They indeed are, as I think Connolly said, incorruptible.

Afterword

RELEASE FROM LONG KESH was traumatic. I remember looking at the closed gates as my comrades drove up to collect me. They had heard through the grapevine - probably through welfare - that I was being turfed out. 'Where do you want to go'? I just looked and we sped off to the Old House Bar in Albert Street, Tommy Slevin's wonderful pub, and my local.

As word spread the bar became crowded, all my old friends were buying drink. The place was jumping. Fortunately I had the good sense to ring my wife Marie. She was living in East Belfast at her old home. Norman Jackson, her father, was a lifelong communist and her mother a member of the Alliance party. They took care of our son Donal while Marie drove over to collect me. It would be years before I could visit them as it was too dangerous at that time: for them and me.

Marie and I left for Dublin on the following day so I could report back to Head Office. But that wasn't the only reason. We wanted to get well away from the murderous environment of Belfast, at least for a while.

Party headquarters then was in Gardiner Place, Dublin. We called in and the late Seán Ó Cionnaith, who was developing an excellent bookshop, told us that Cathal Goulding, Liam Mc Millen and Seán Garland were in Stoney Burke's bar around the corner in Hill Street. Their welcome was heart-warming. Liam McMillen was in great form – he was 'on the run' from Northern Ireland. Sadly Liam would soon be dead: murdered sitting beside his wife Mary on on Belfast's Falls Road. His killer was Gerard Steenson, a young man whom I had recruited at the request of his father, a former member of the Northern Ireland Labour Party. Steenson was part of Seamus Costello's gang and was responsible for many foul murders. I was lucky: he tried to shoot me in Mary Dowds' house in Plevna Park, Belfast. Flinging myself across a little room I half blocked the kitchen door, his firing was indiscriminate almost killing Mary as well as myself.

As I have already said Marie and I wanted away from Belfast so we headed first for Connemara. We had been there years before and were glad to return but we also wanted to say hello to Ireland's champion tin whistle player, from Spideal who had often played in Tommy Slevin's bar, Festy Conlon. We carried on after leaving Festy promising to return and made our way to Ceathru Rua (Carraroe) in the heart of the Connemara Gaeltacht. I wanted to call into the pub-hotel where Derek Peters and I had stayed.

While their names now elude me, I can still recall and hear the terror their mother had felt when we had gone fishing with one of her sons. As a gale blew, she spent the afternoon on her knees praying: 'my son knows as much about the sea as a Connemara donkey'! On visiting once more they asked us to stay but we went onwards to the Gaeltacht Hotel. Very up-market. We then headed further North to Donegal, our favourite county, to meet more old friends the McGeehans, near Fintona. We had a drink together in Meli's Bar, spent the night, then faced up to the vicious reality of returning to blood soaked Northern Ireland.

And that's what it was.

THE MURDEROUS SECTARIAN Nationalist and Loyalist rampages are well known and documented. Between them they gouged the heart out of Northern Ireland. Crimes committed 'in the pursuit of freedom' or the 'defence of liberty'. From the Shankhill Butchers to the Enniskillen bombers we witnessed Northern Ireland sink into a stinking morass of evil and virtual total despair.

Those who boasted their republican credentials, such as Adams and McGuinness knew nothing of Tone's Unity of Protestant, Catholic and Dissenter. On the contrary they were the bitter, fundamental causes and pursuers of division. That cannot be denied.

We are a deeply divided sectarian entity. According to the recent Northern Ireland Peace Monitoring Report we have forty eight 'Peace Walls'. The number keeps growing. We make the once infamous Berlin Wall look like a sick joke. That is the tragedy of our times: a population that apparently thrives on hate and bile. Our culture is dark, ugly and grotesque. Love and divinity are missing from the lives, of even those who believe in such concepts. It would be all too easy to let go into despair. But to deny happiness, to see Northern Ireland as an absolutely failed sectarian province would be to award victory to those who had always sought this. It would also be to ignore the good people who wanted integrated education, housing and employment. For my part I cannot and will not do that. This is the reason I am writing this postscript.

We must invoke the spirit and courage of the Civil Rights Movement. There is no going back, that is impossible. But we can go forward. Would that I could write with conviction that it would be together. But that will only be the case for those who have common principles, ideals and goals.

For me and my comrades, that is encapsulated in the Workers Party. We have fought many battles against sectarianism and terrorism. We have suffered defections from within our ranks, for personal gain or the love of the whiff of cordite. We will face further hard struggles in the year ahead. But we will not flinch.

The Party's ranks are open to all those who subscribe to our ideals and who will fight for the goal of a democratic, secular, socialist republic on the island of Ireland.

D O'H